Unicorns and Mermaids Adult Coloring Book

This Coloring book belongs to:

____

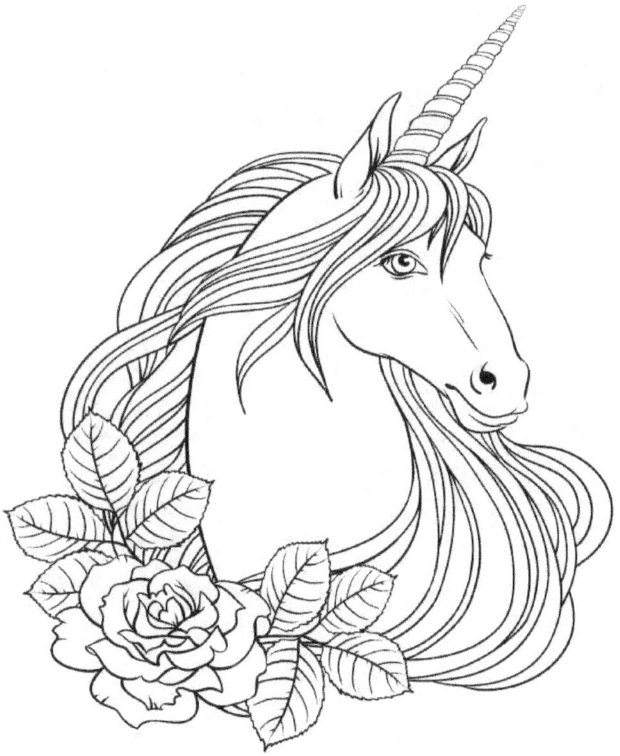

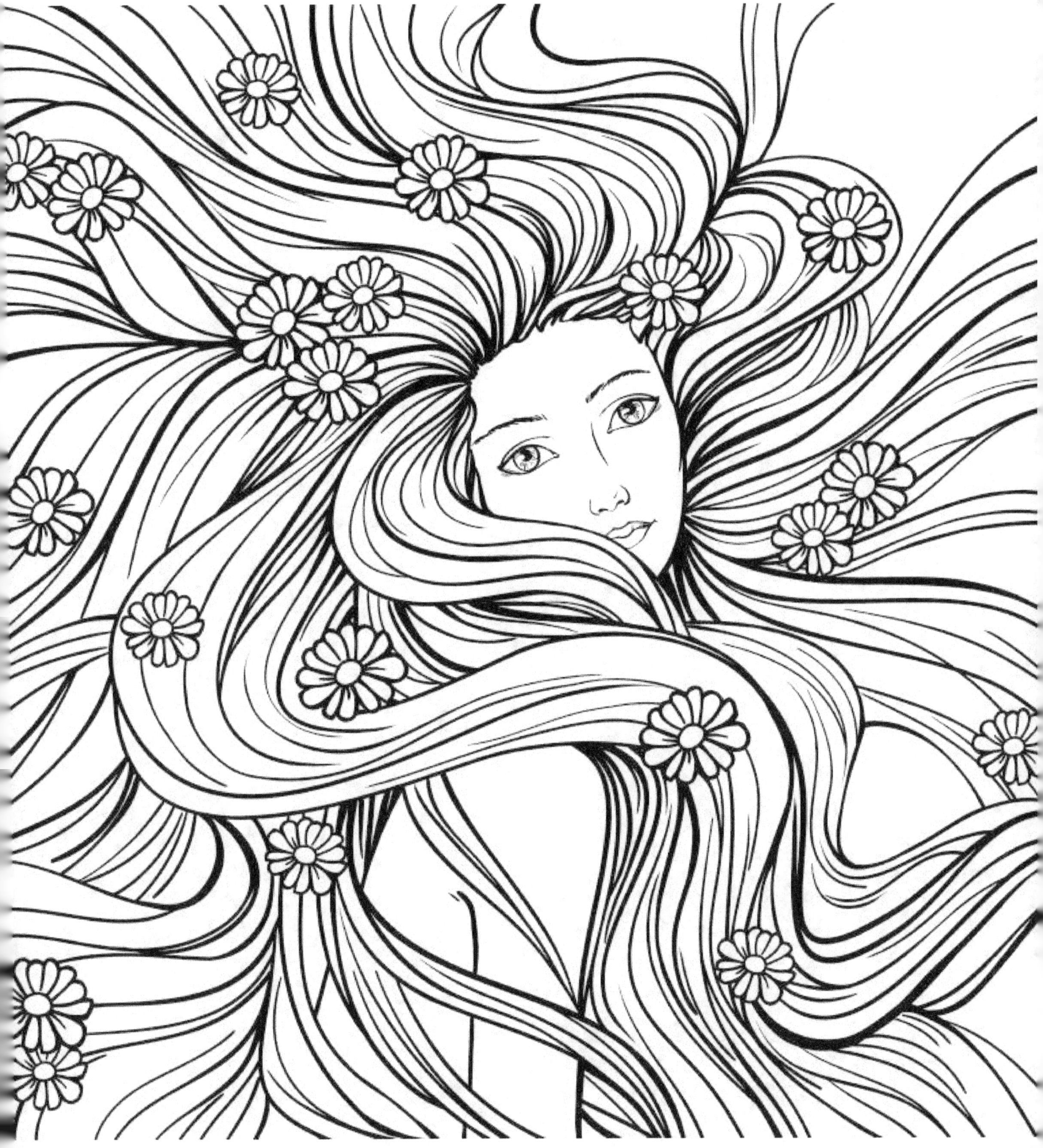

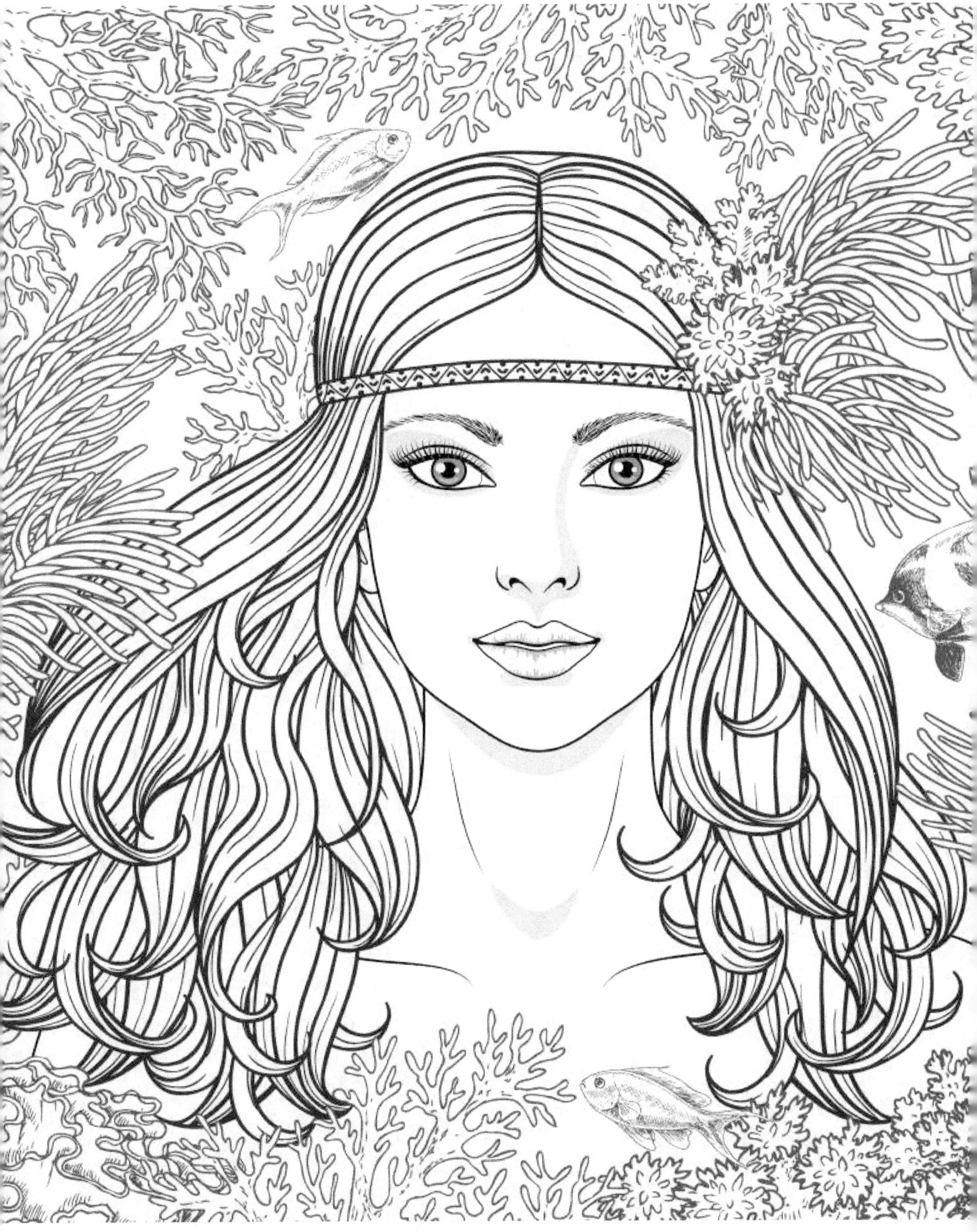

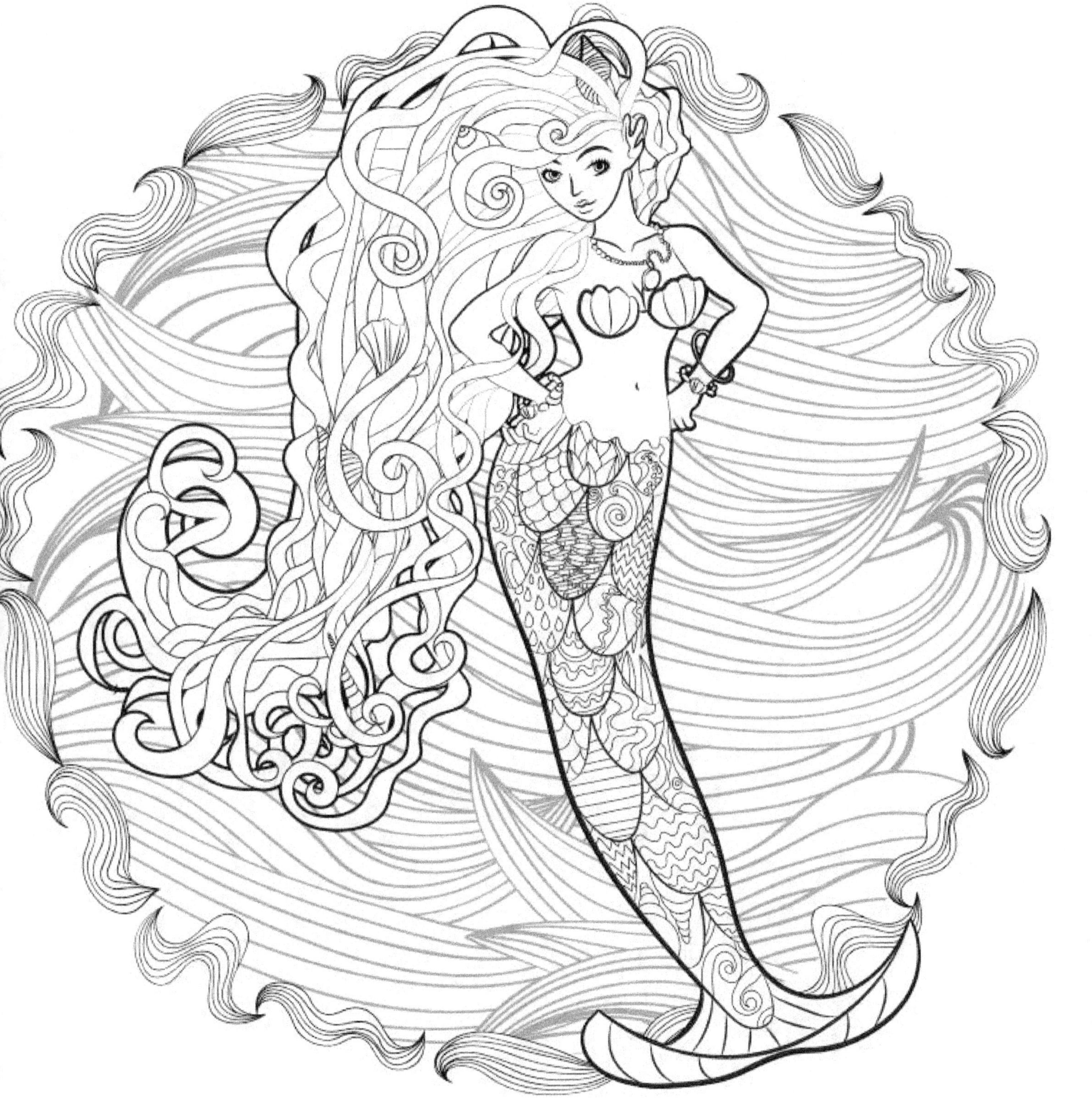

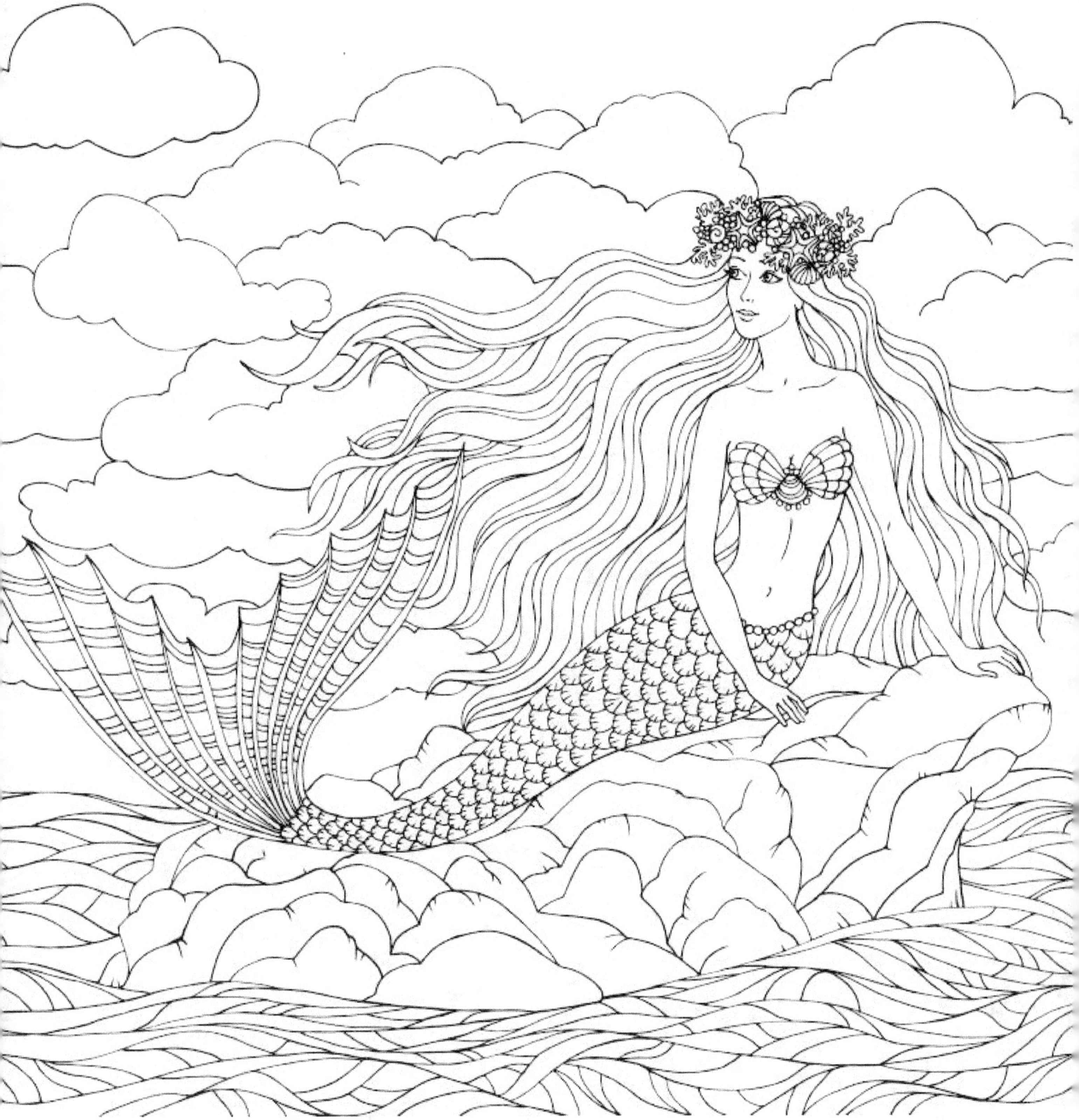

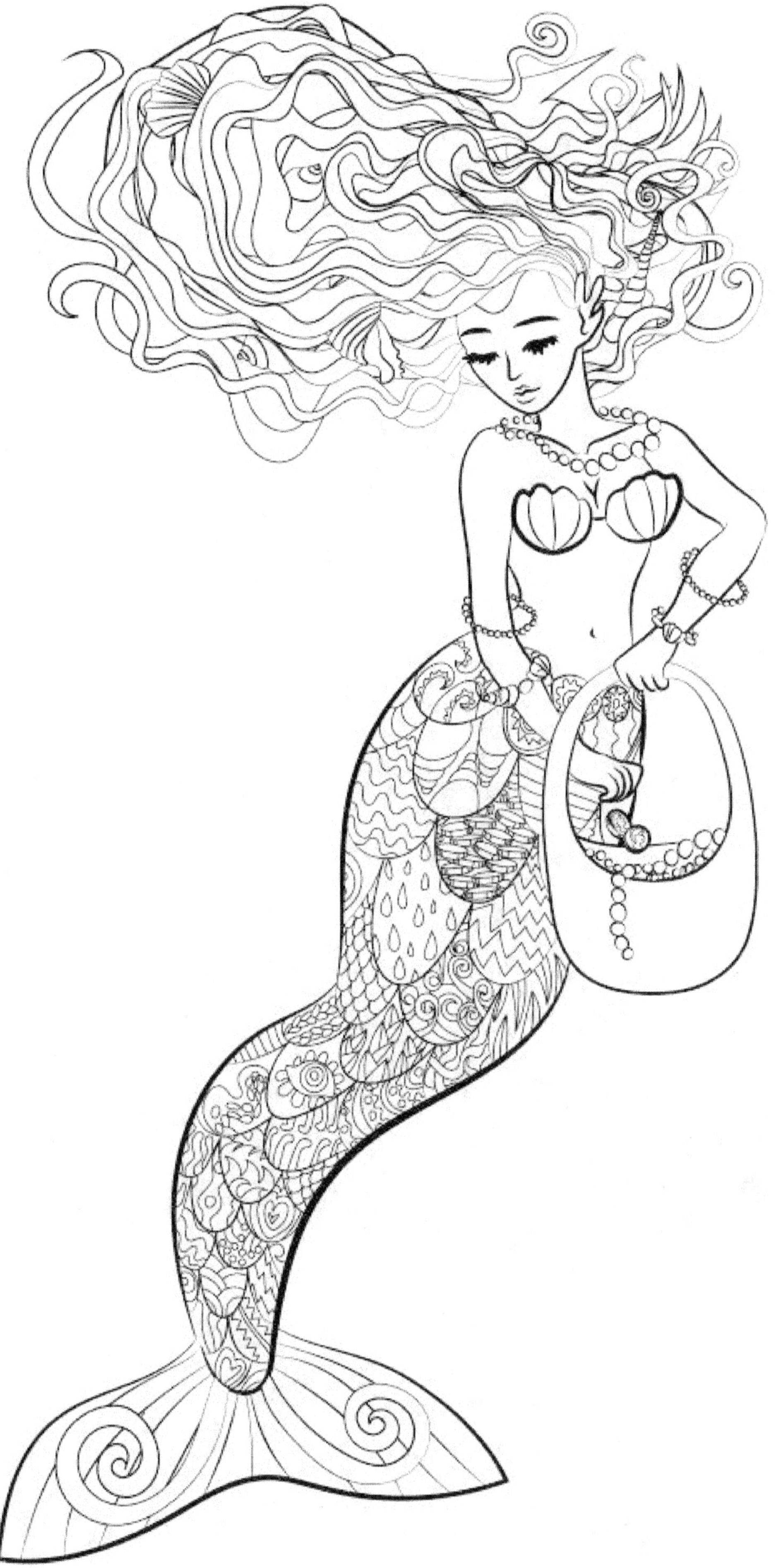

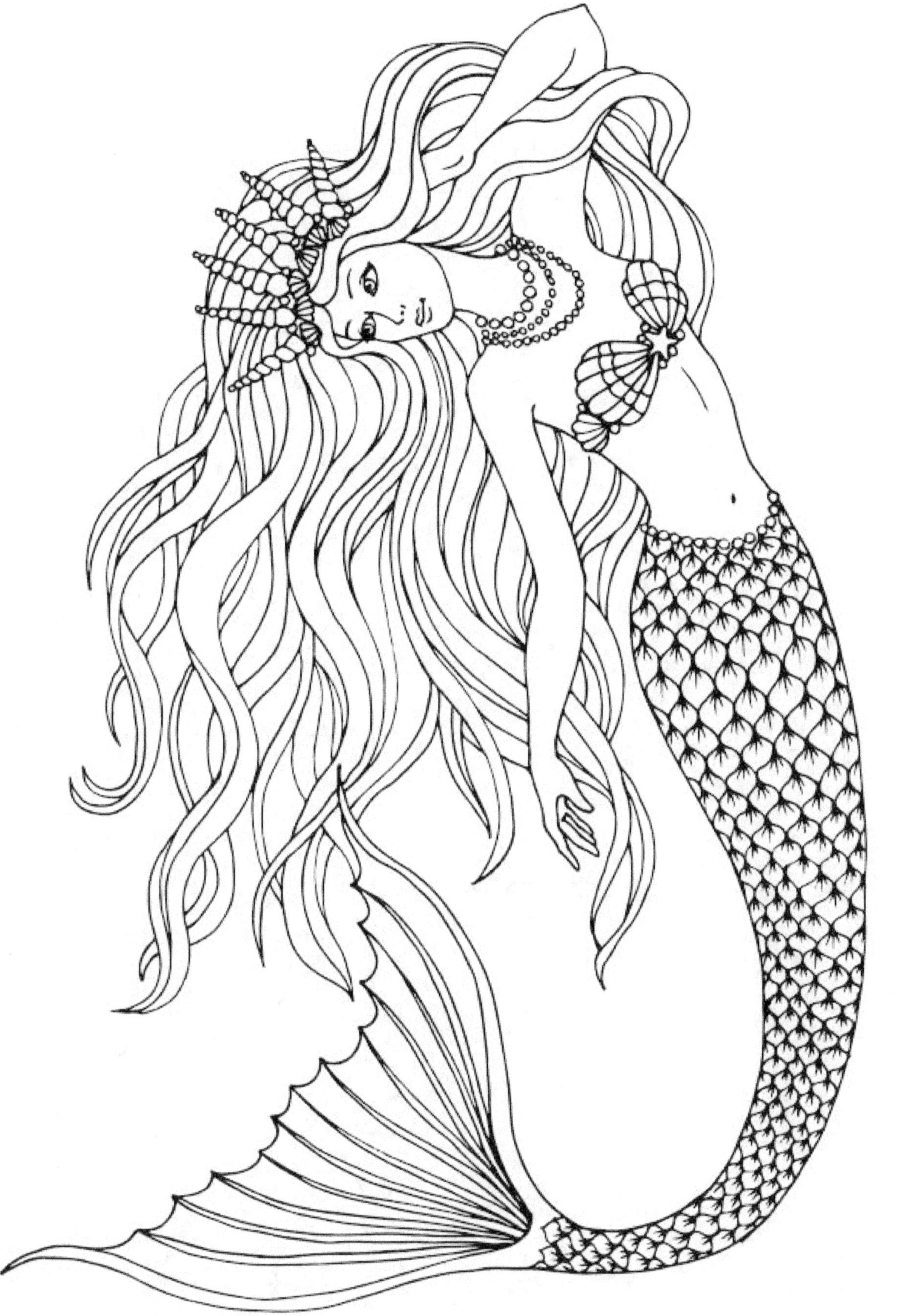

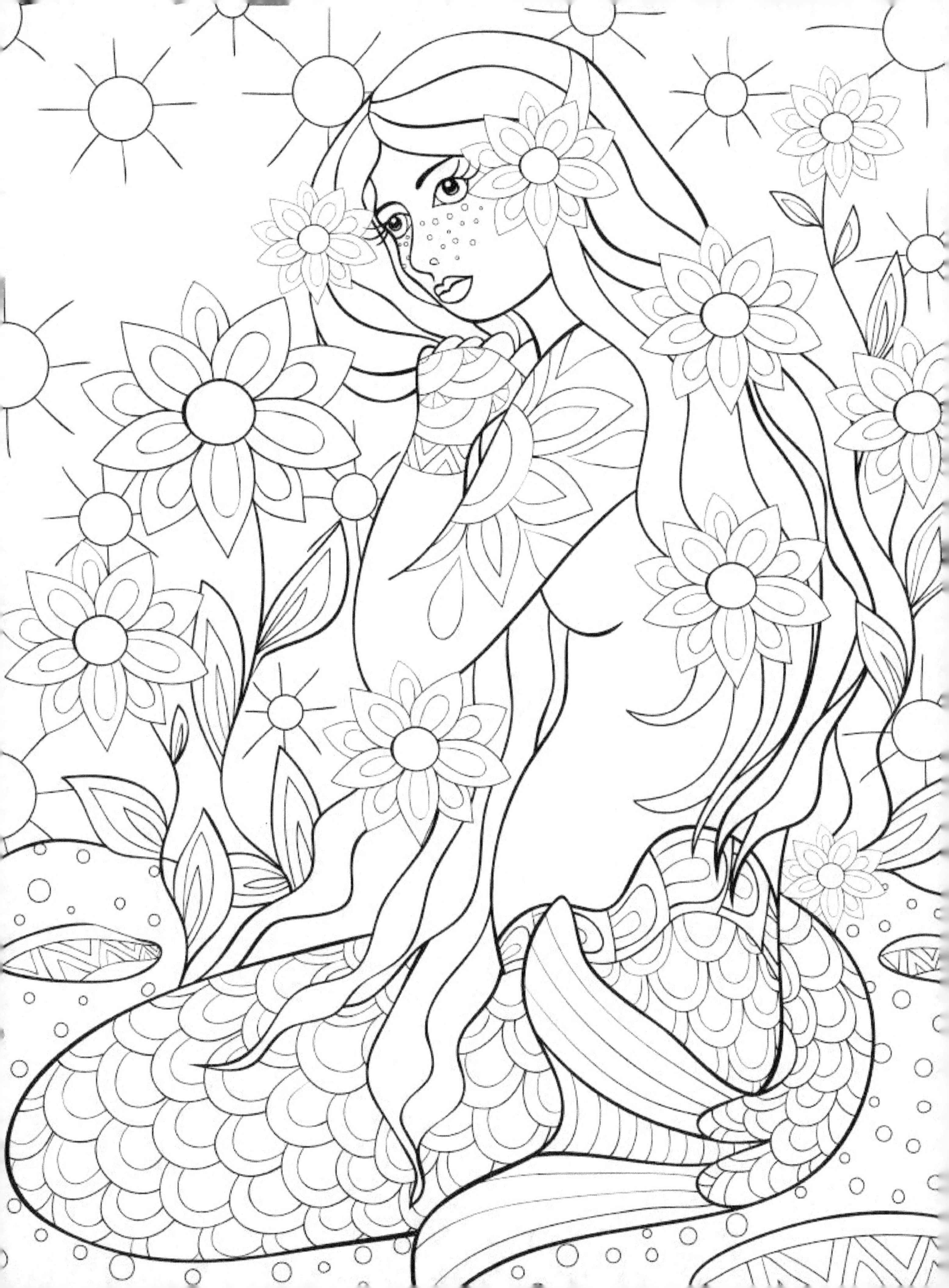

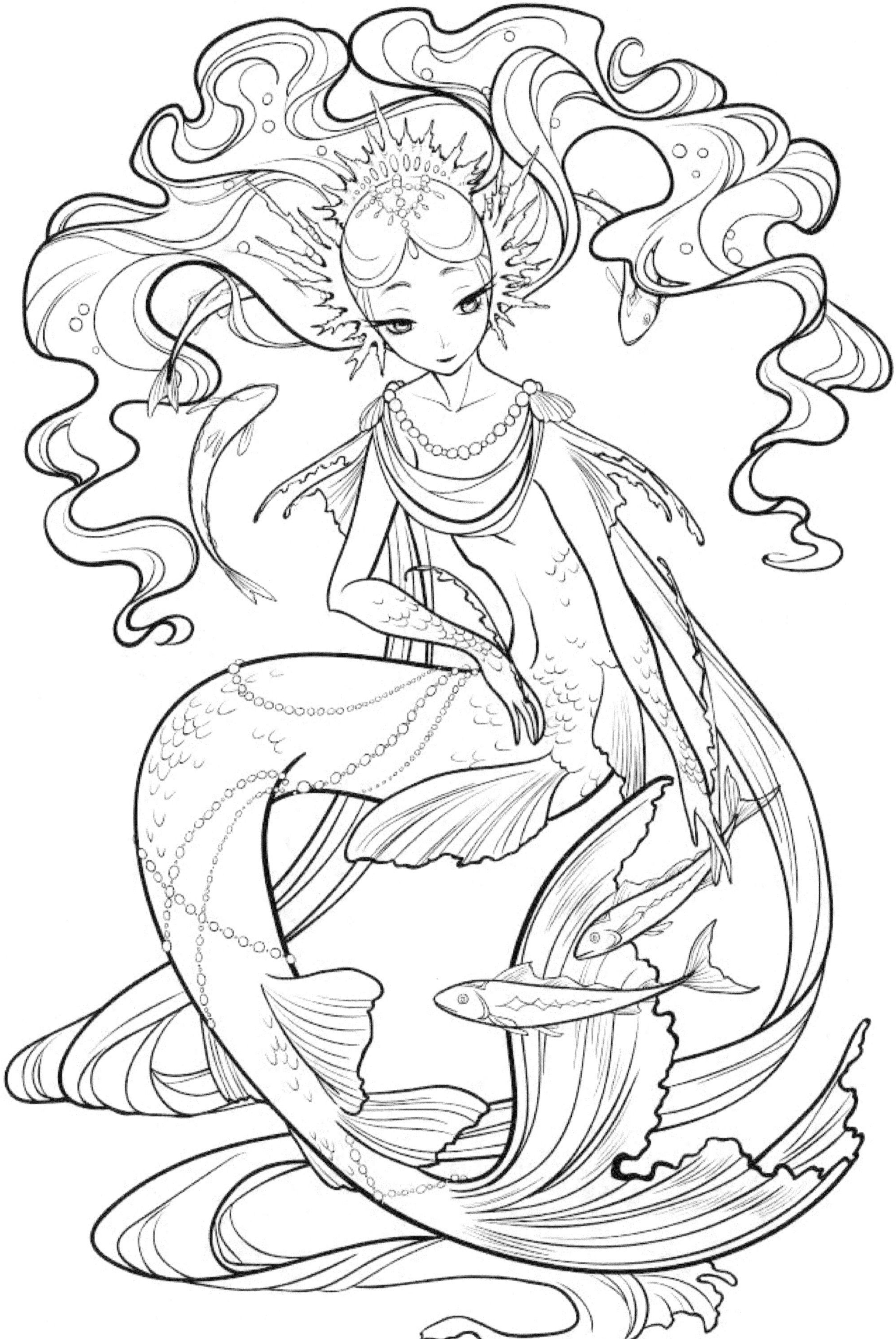

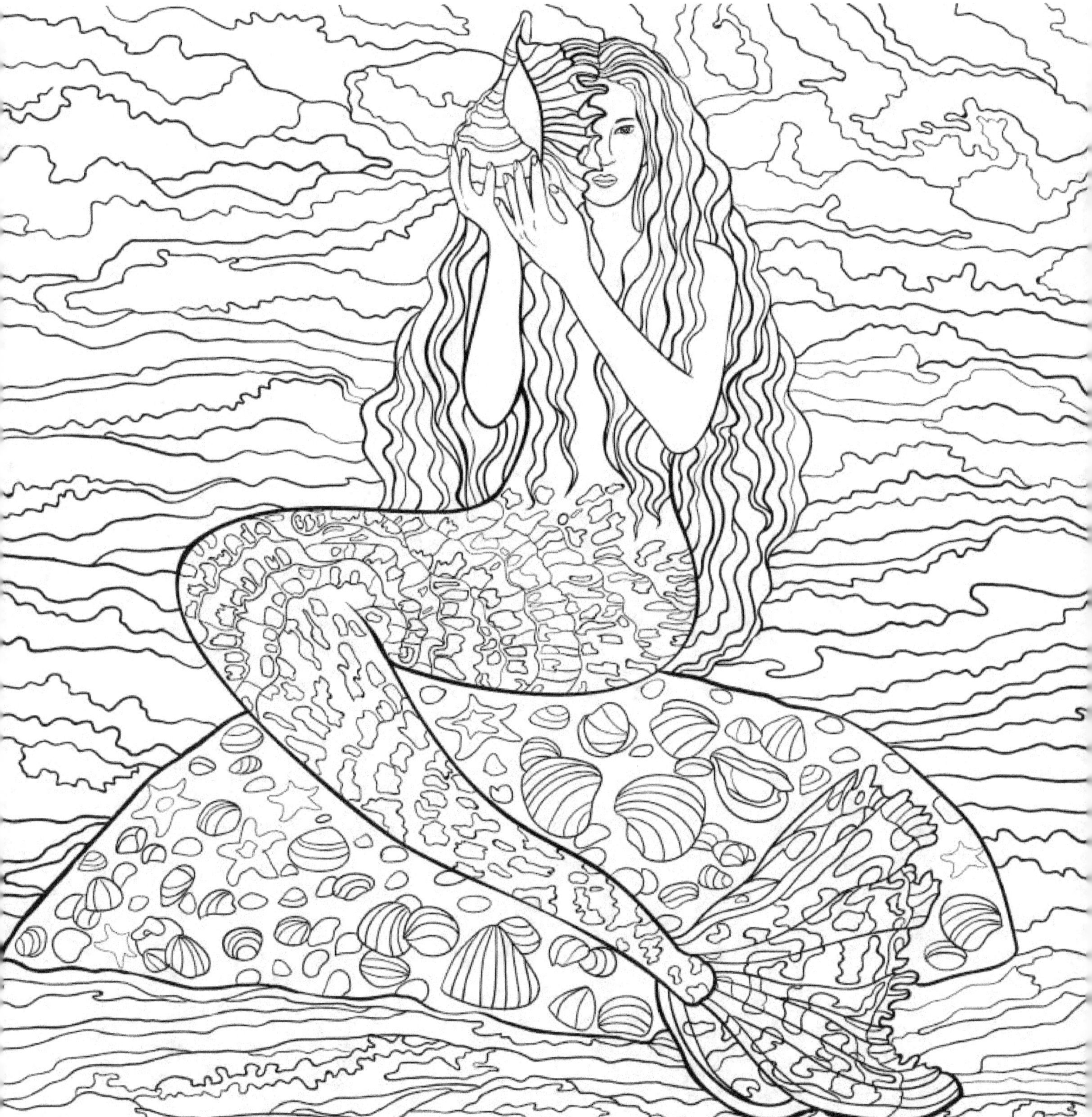

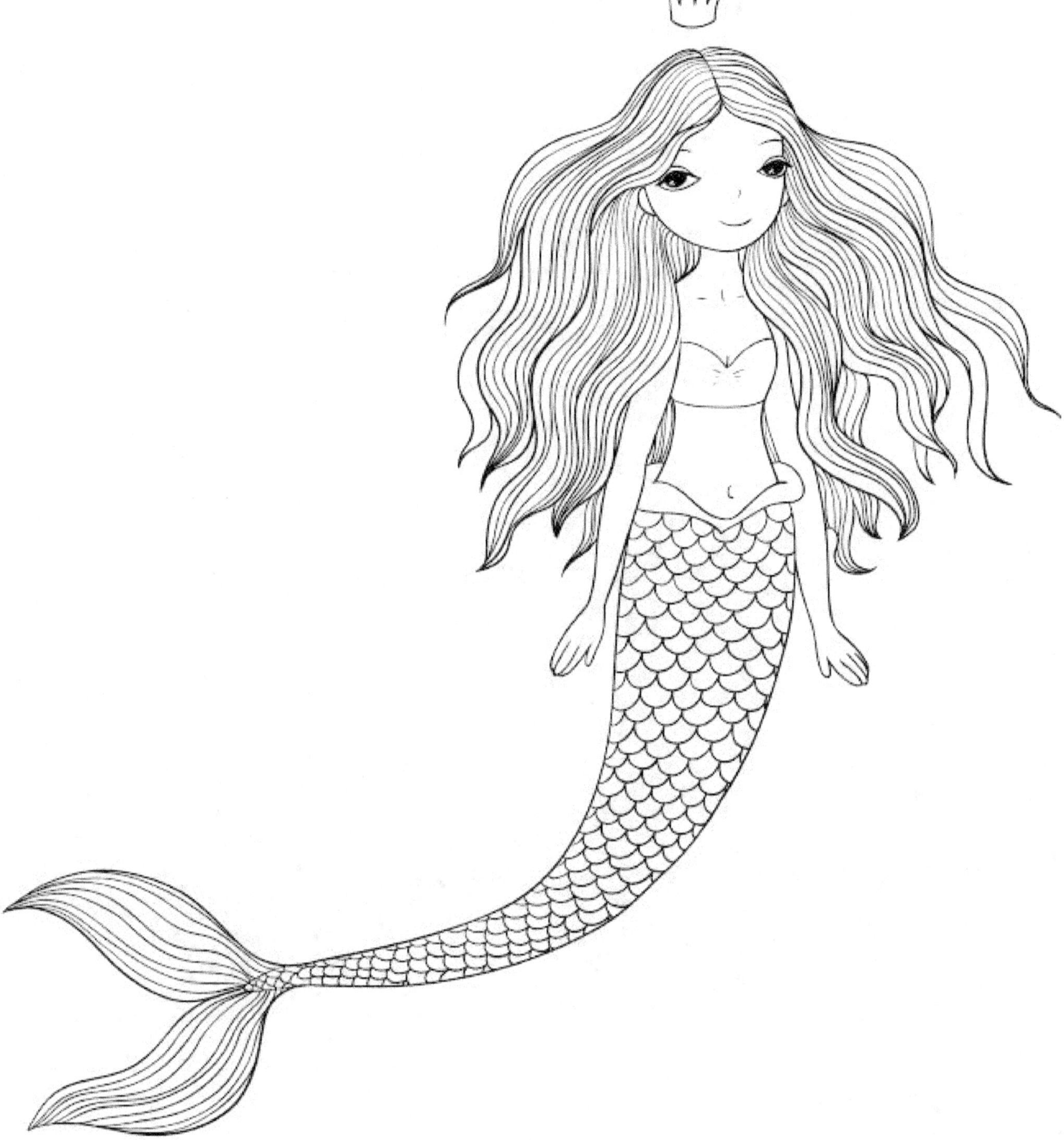

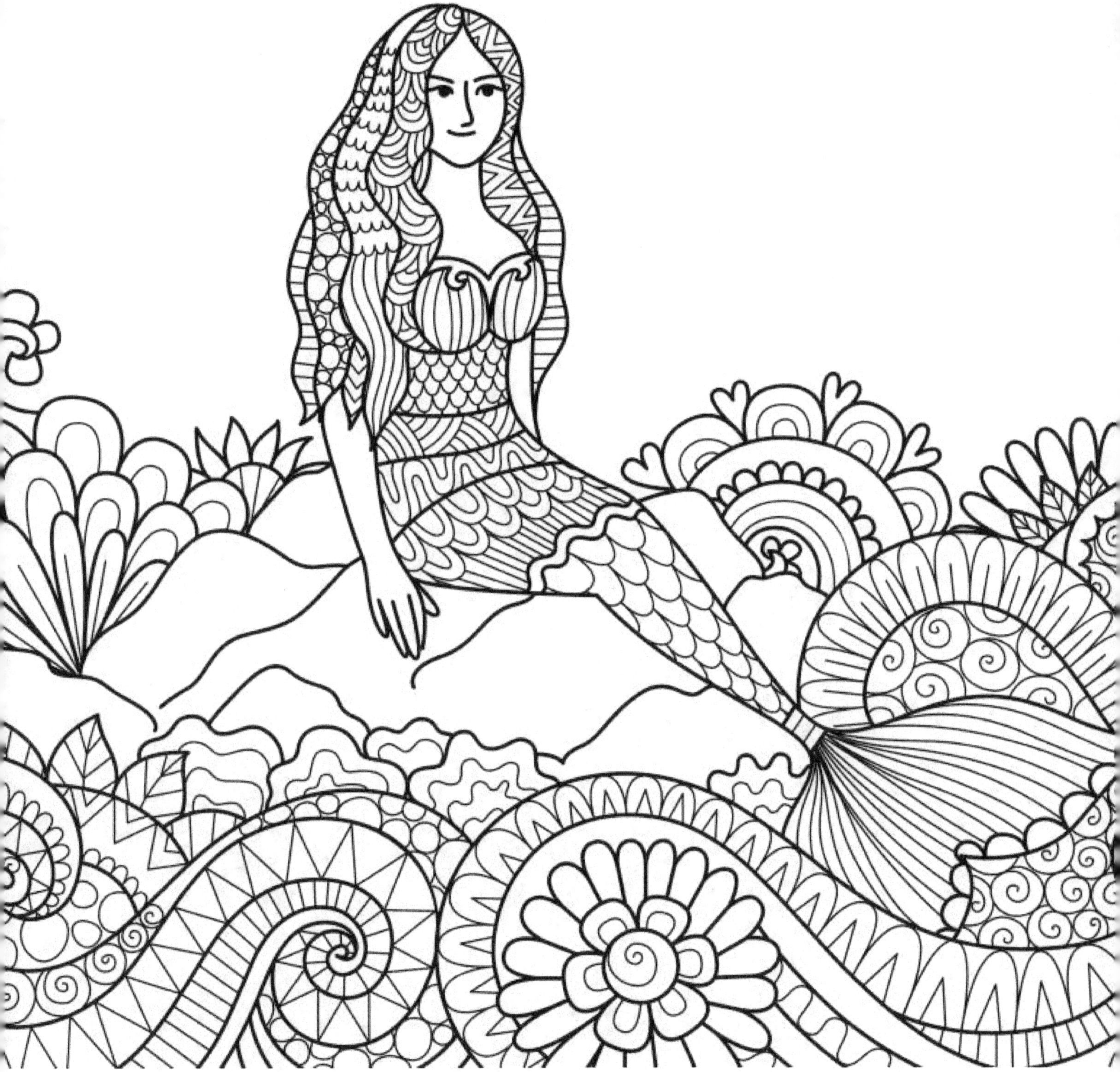

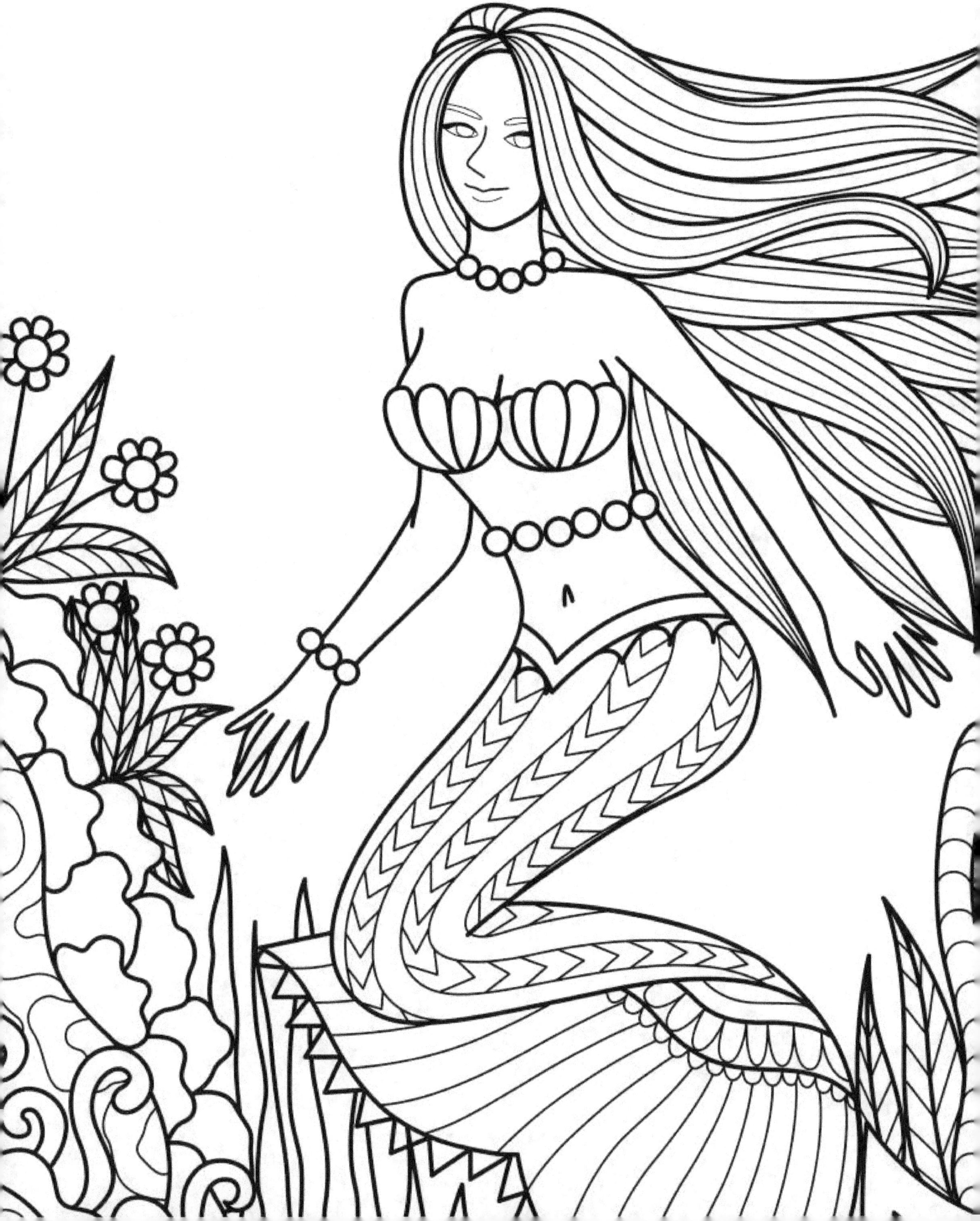

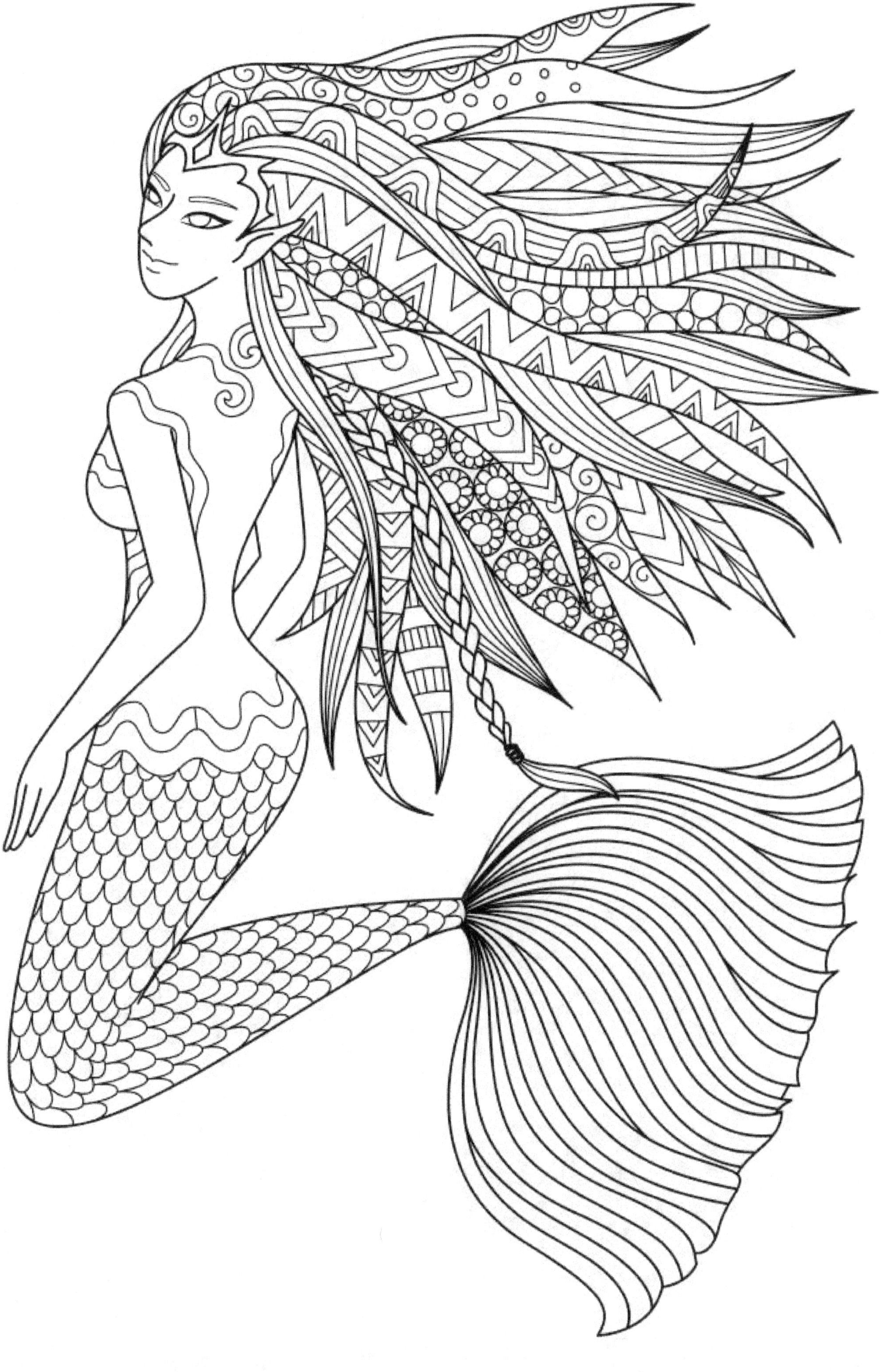

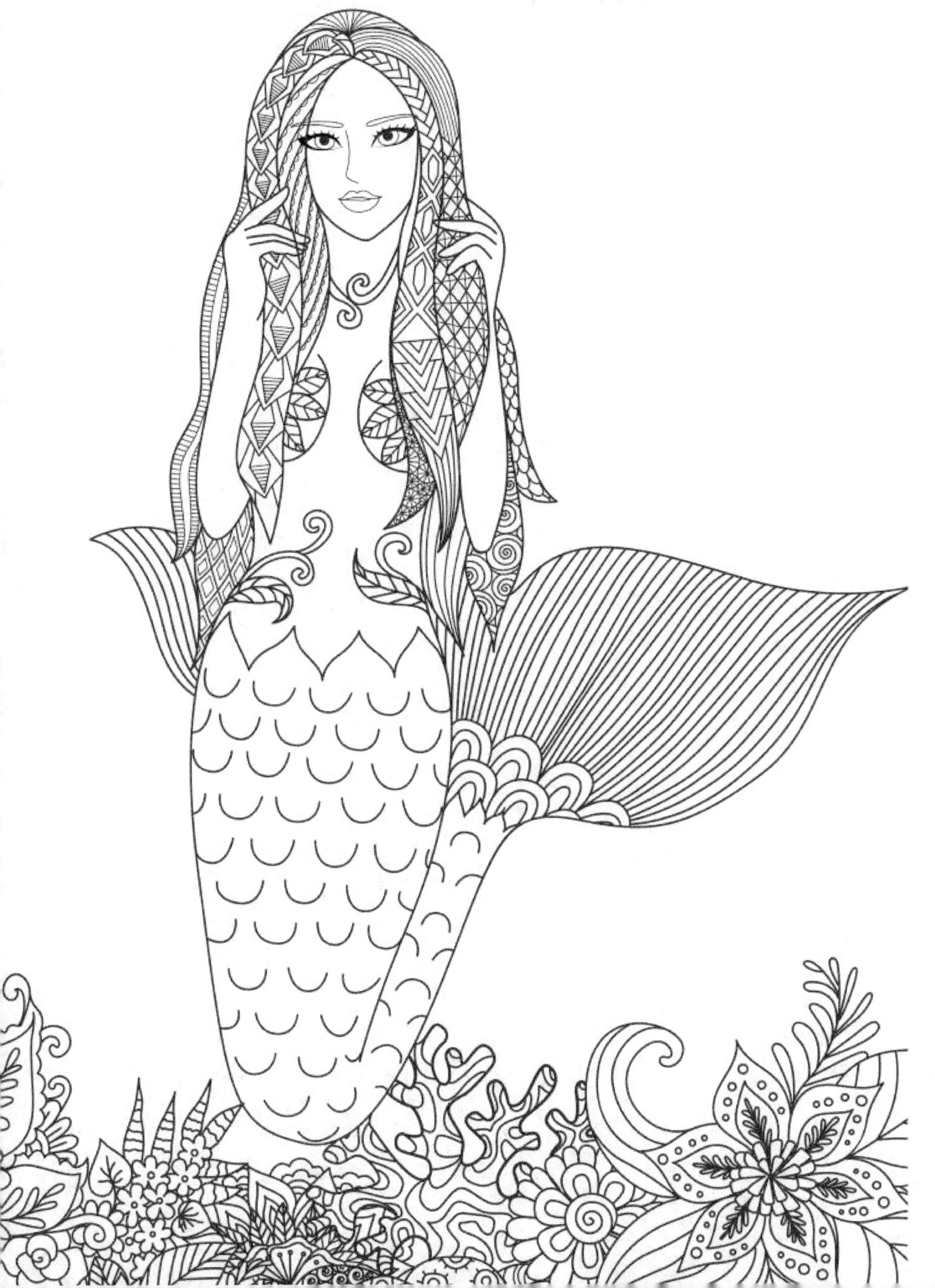

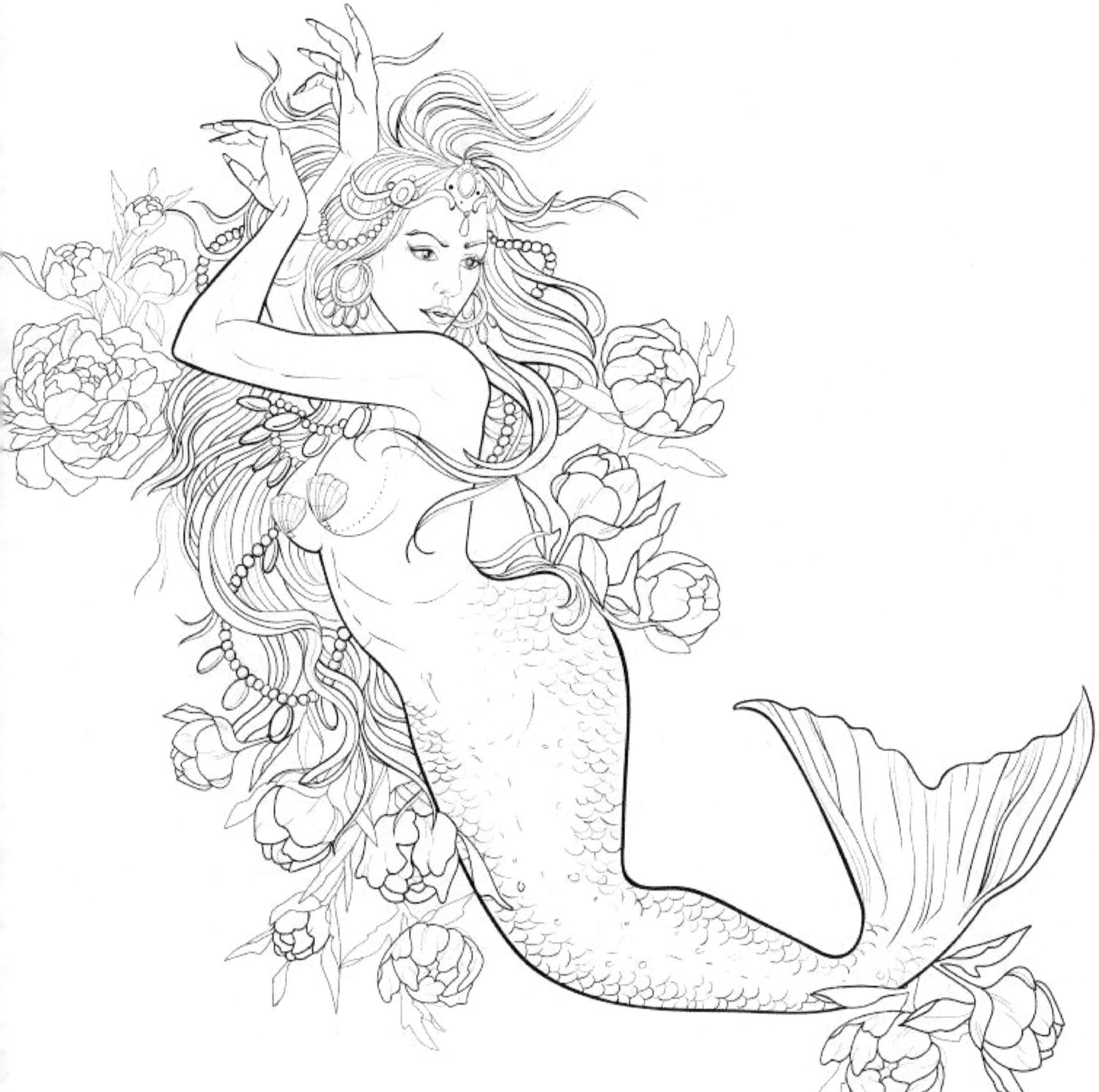

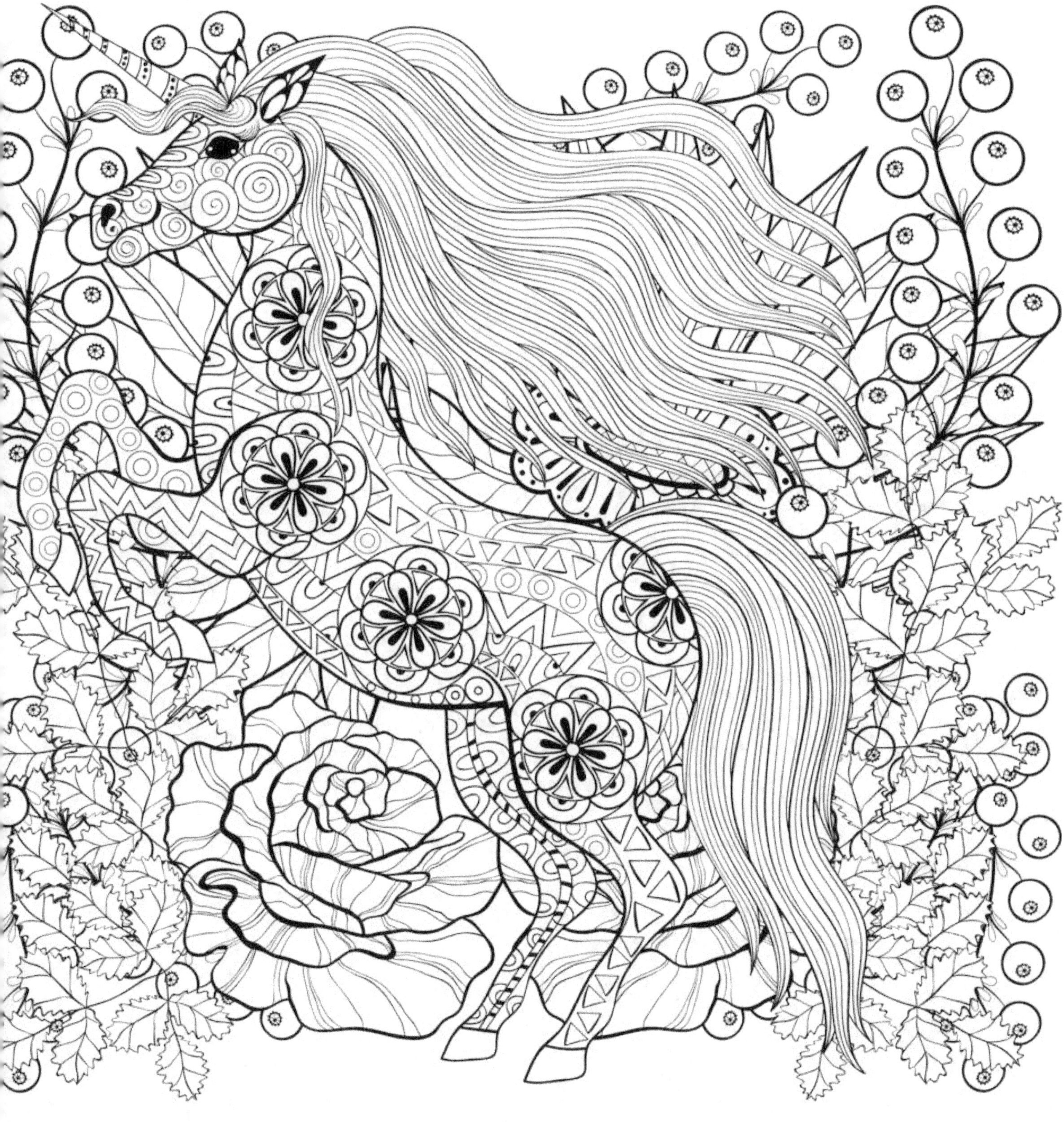

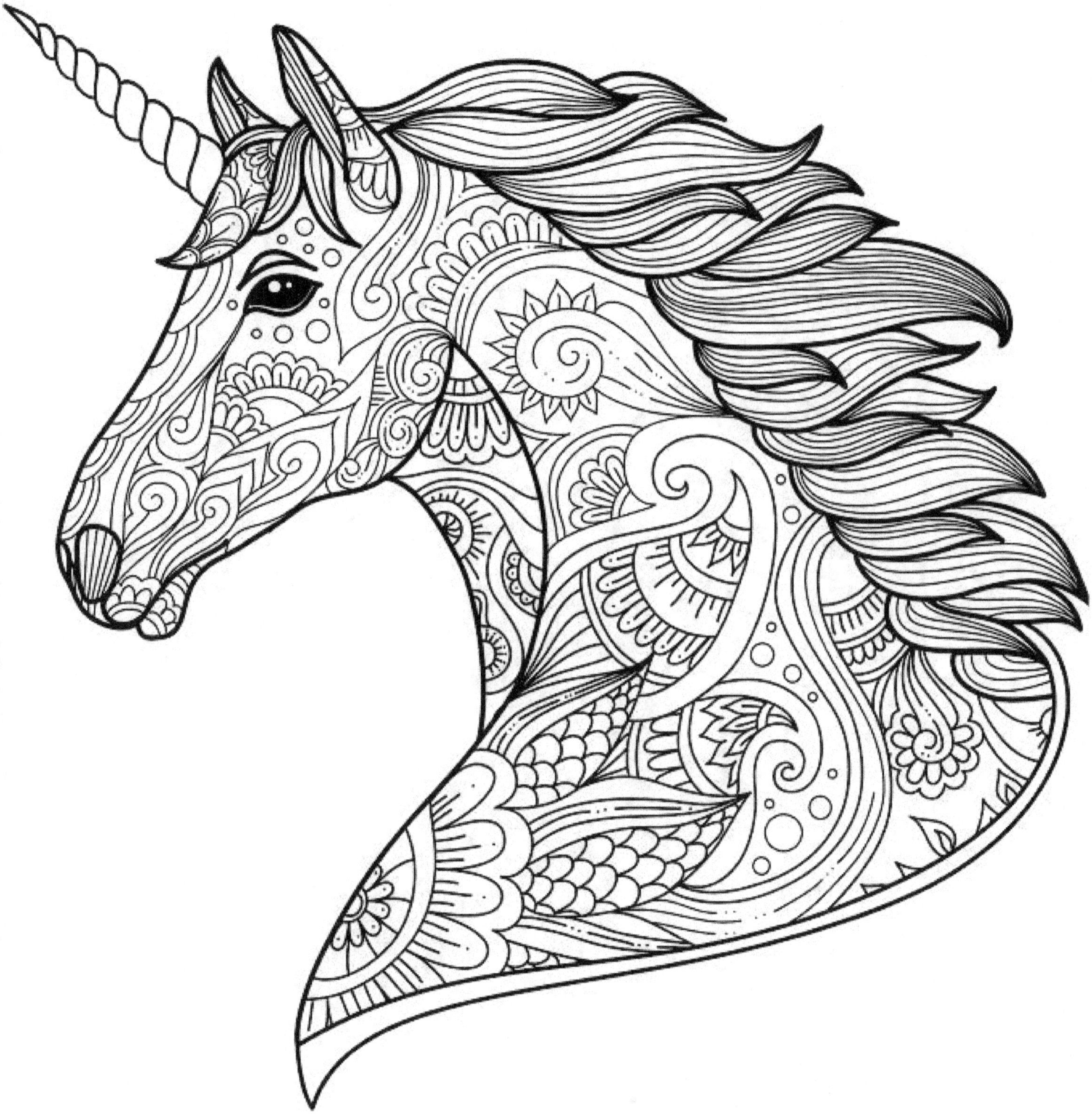

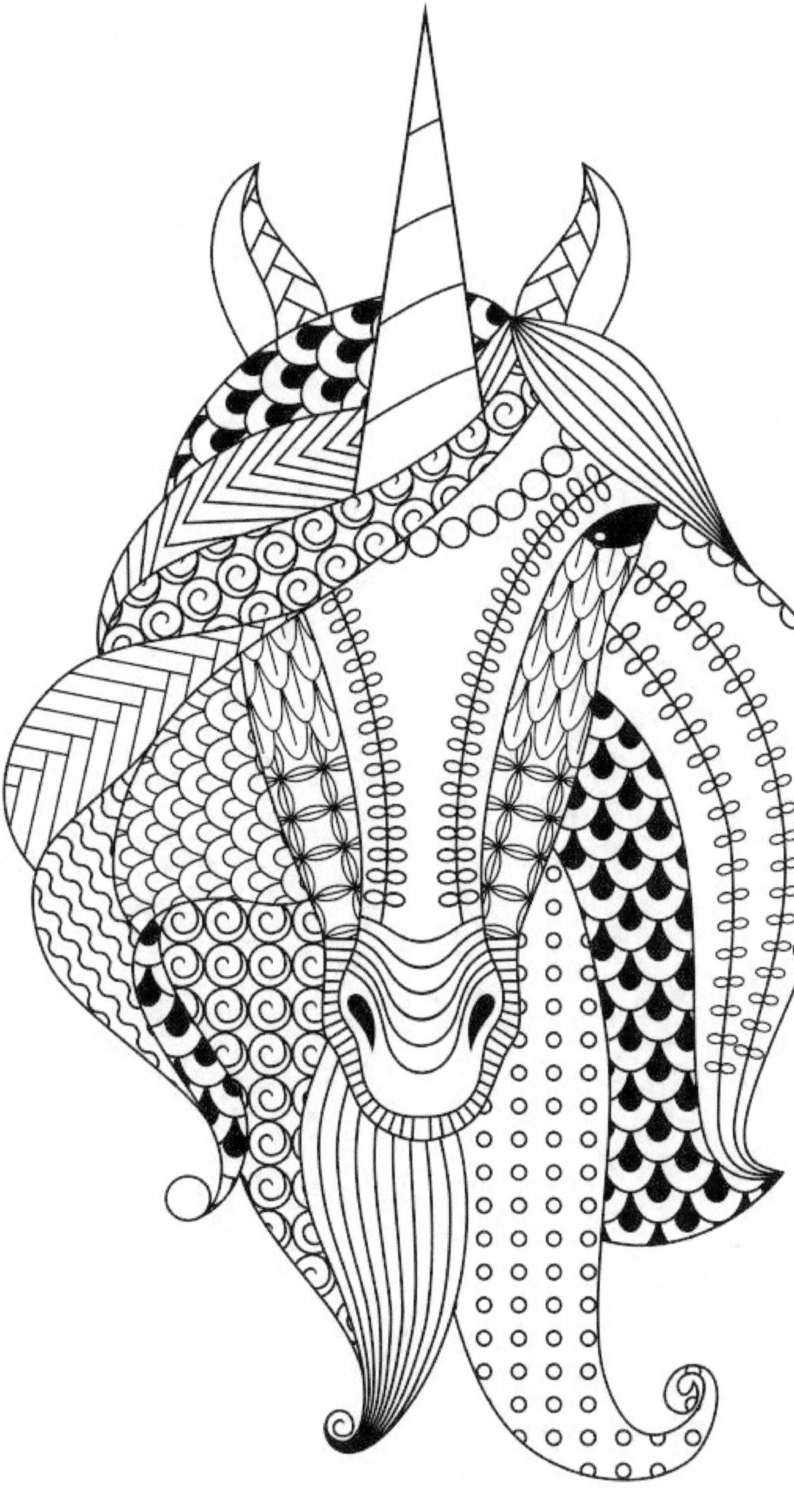

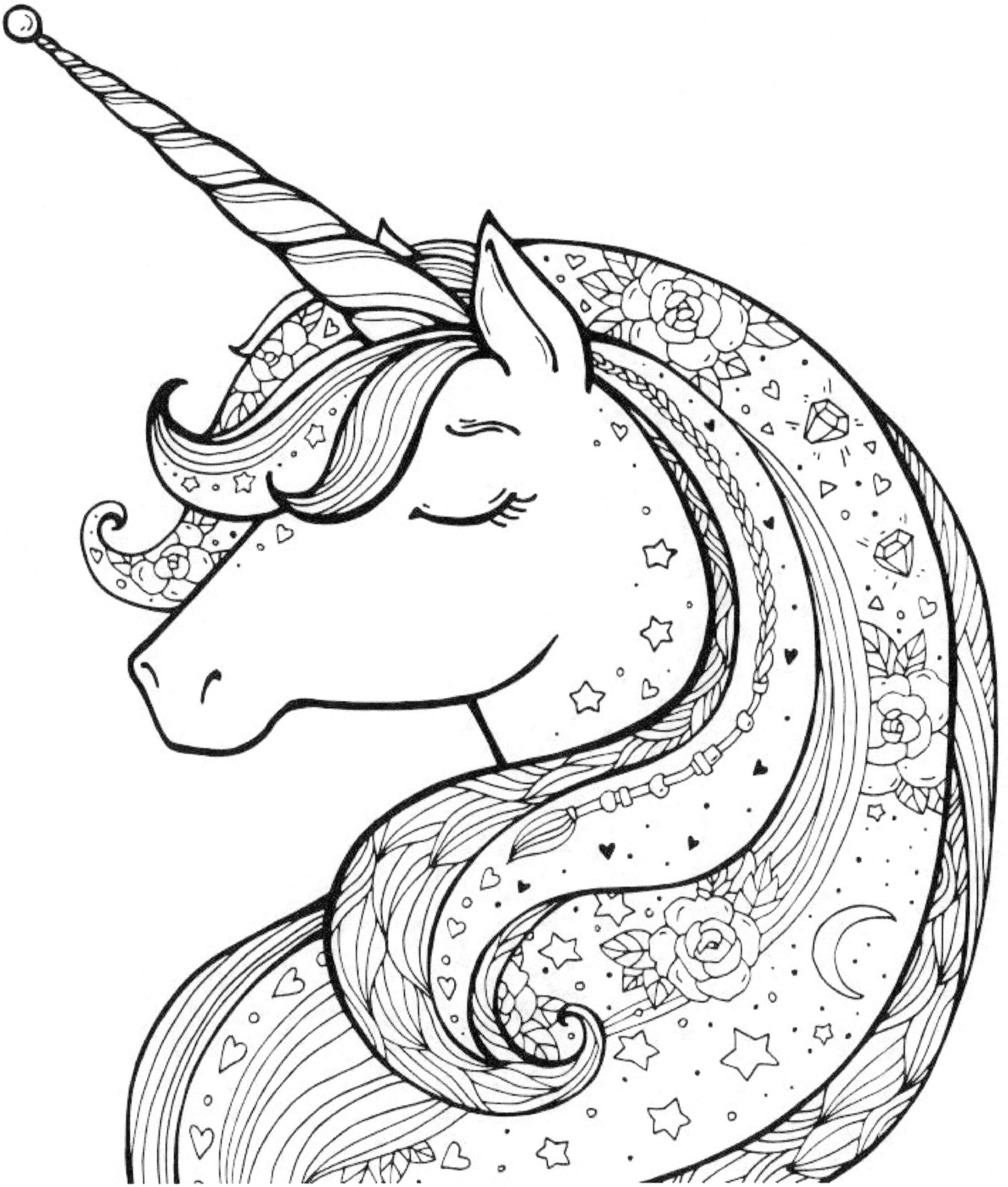

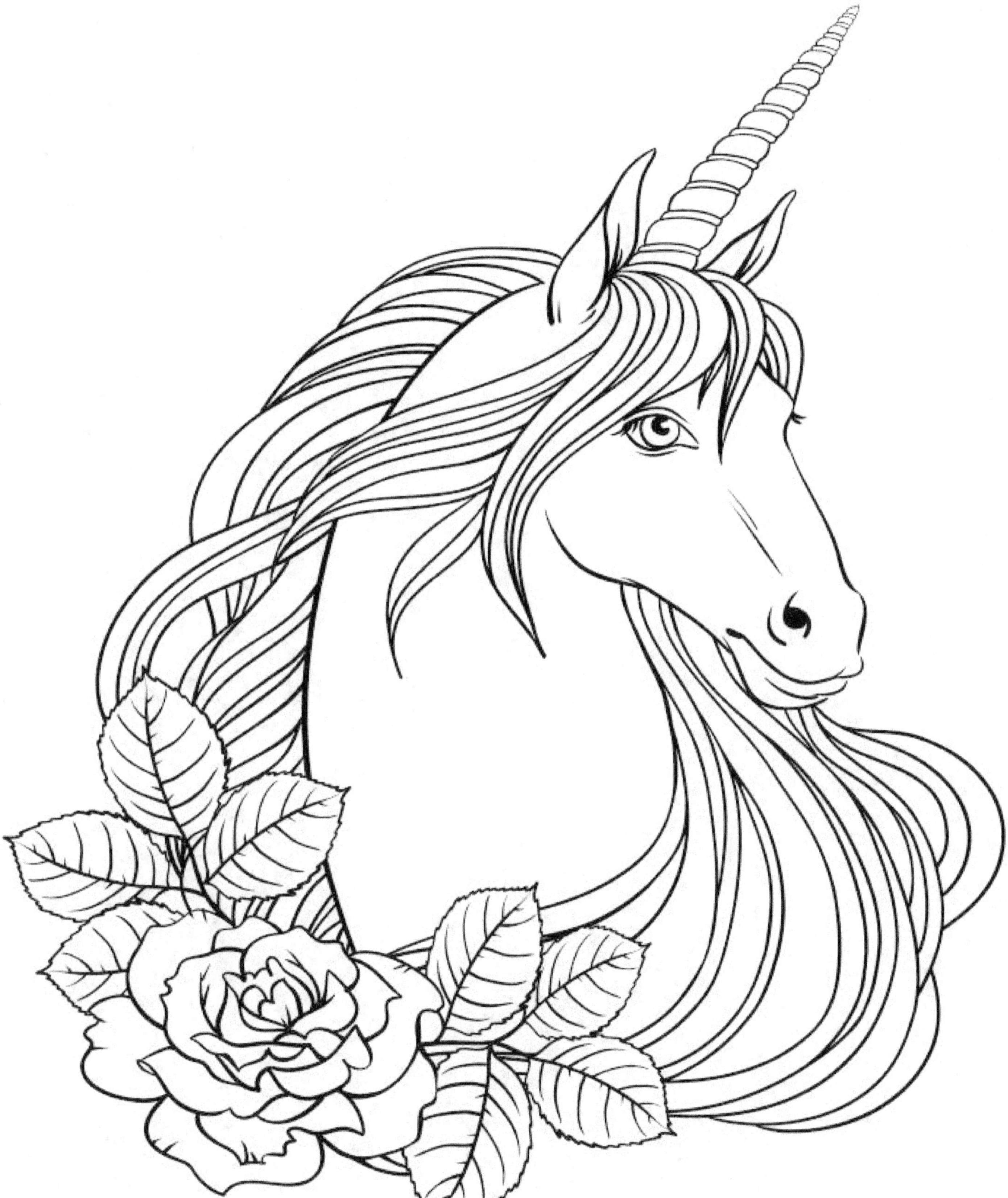

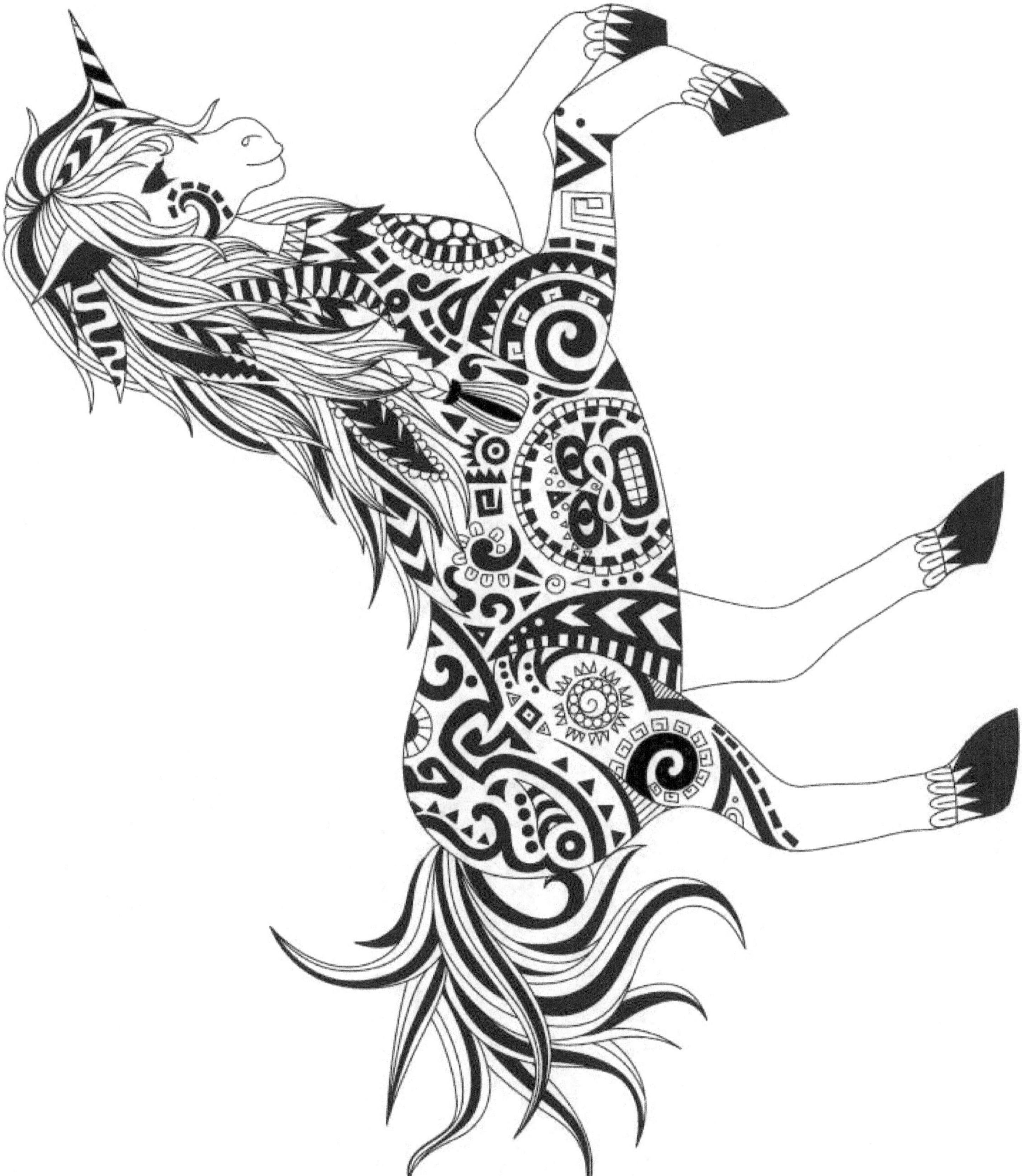

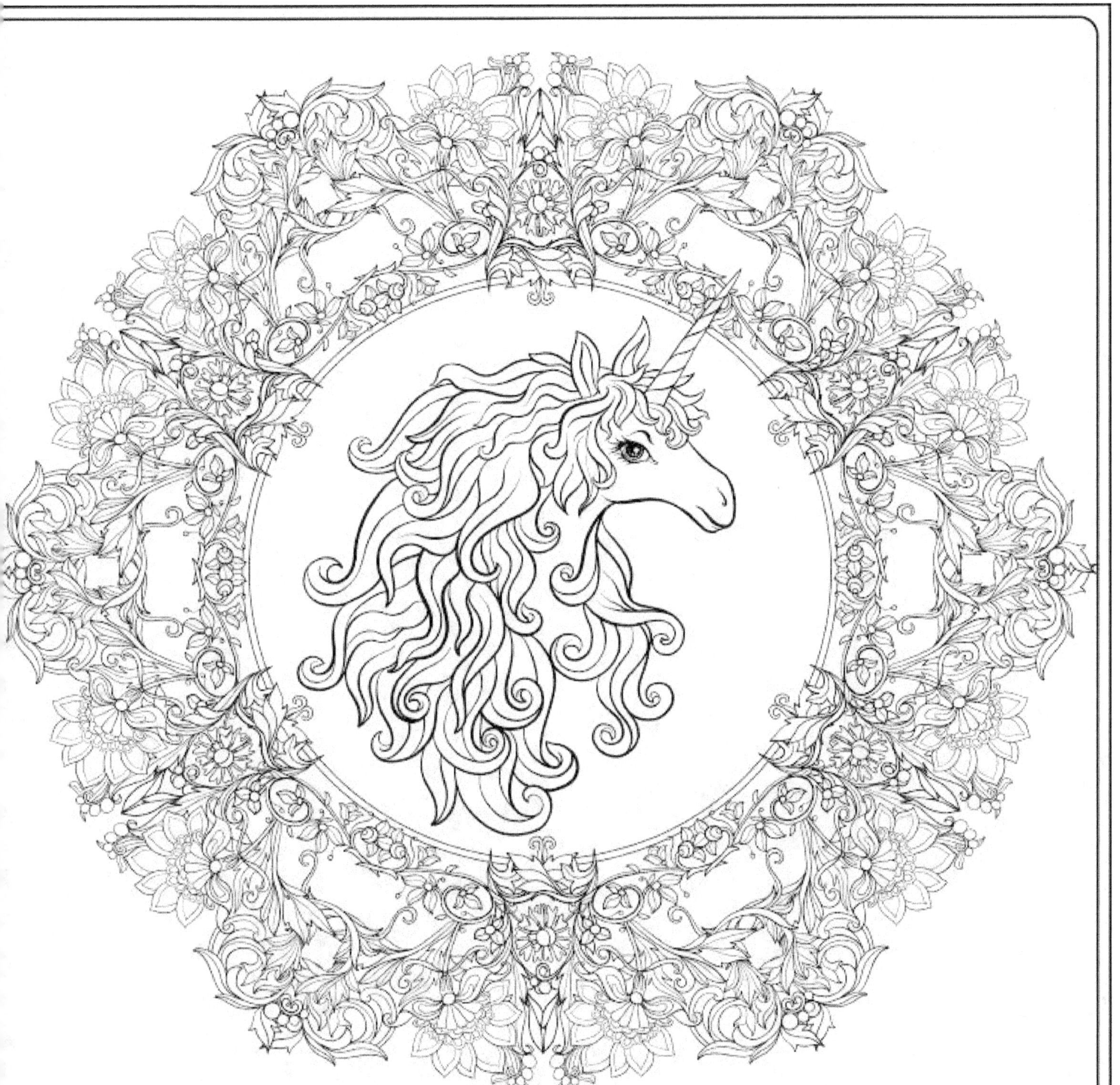

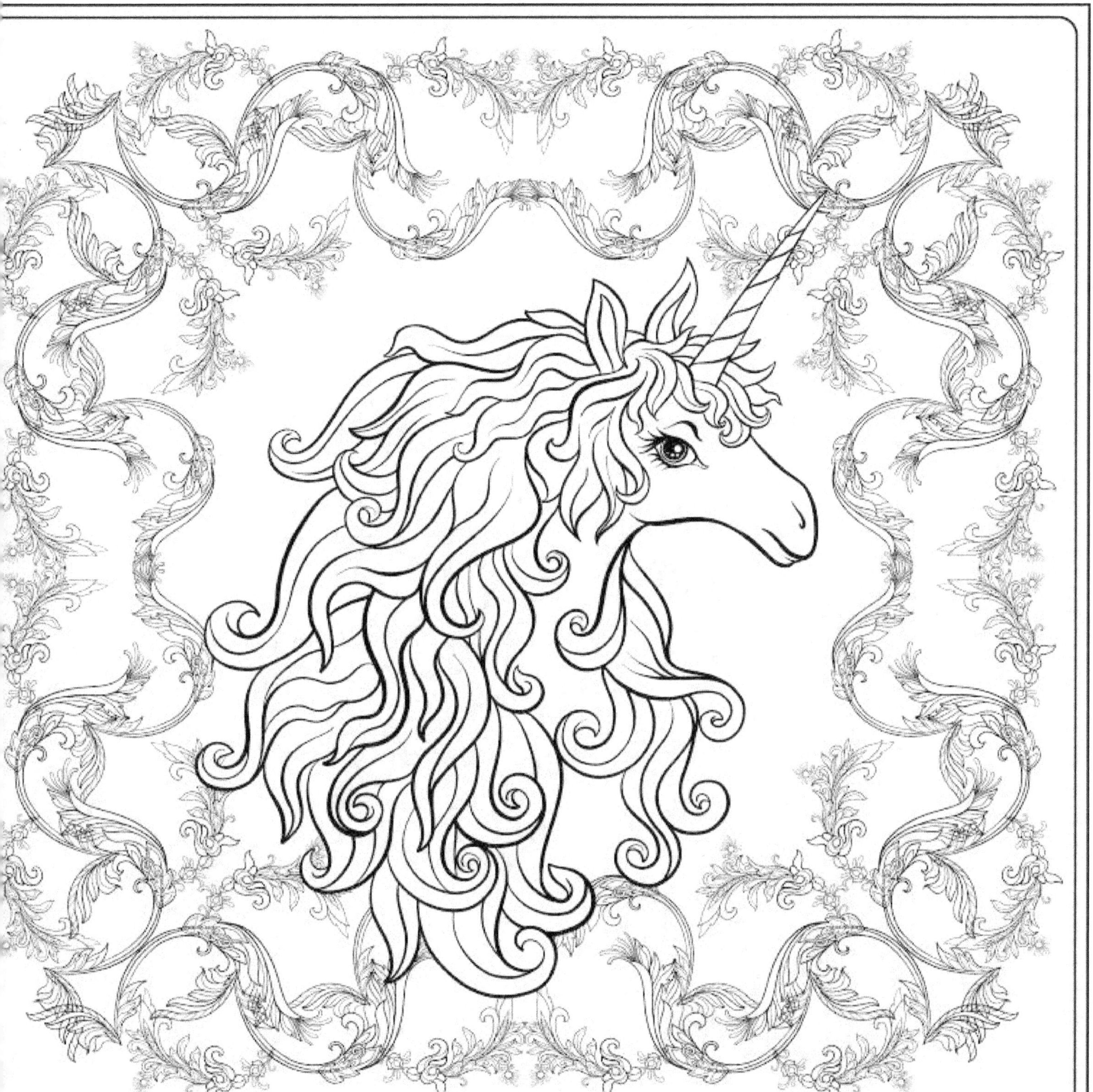

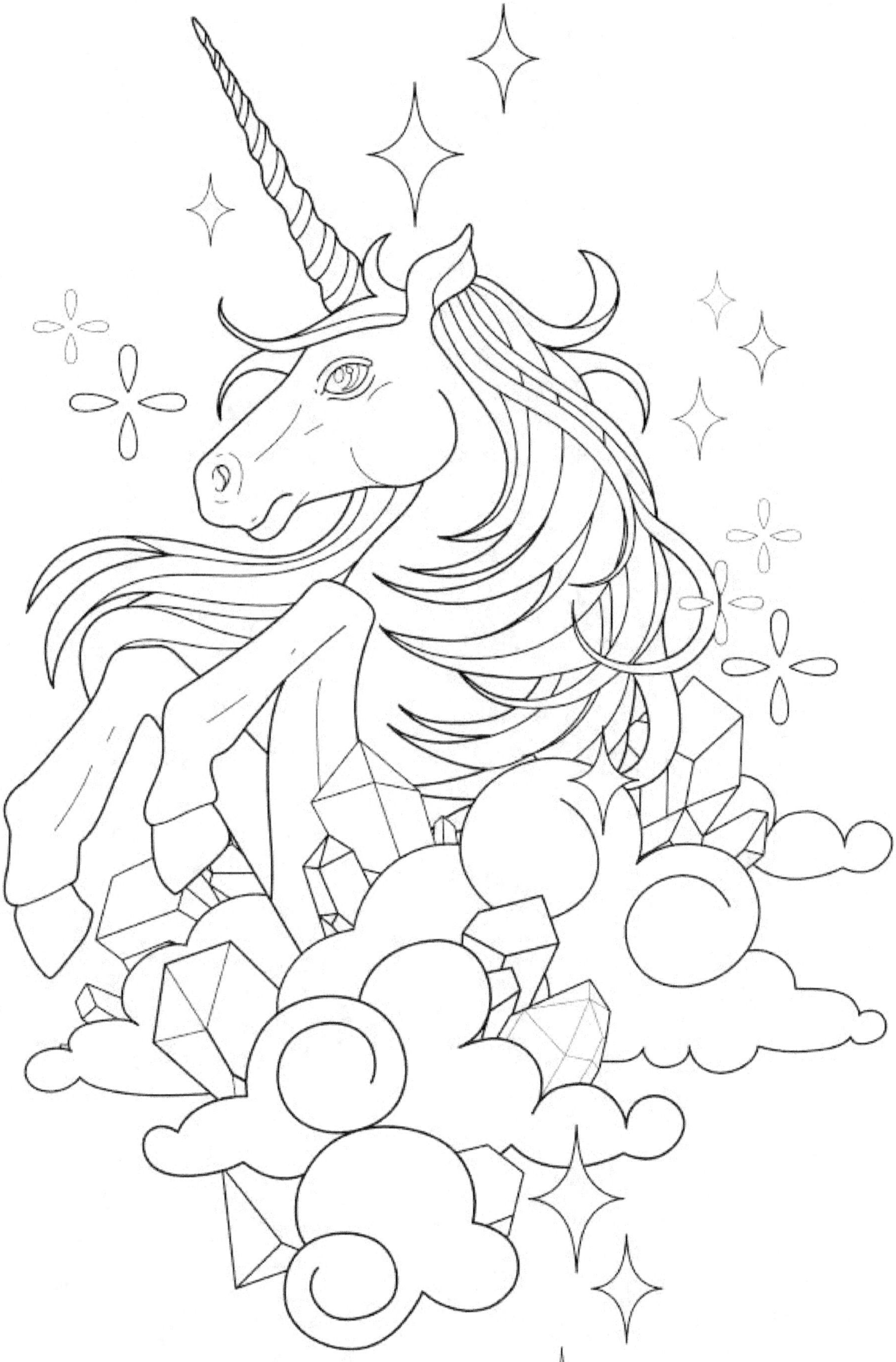

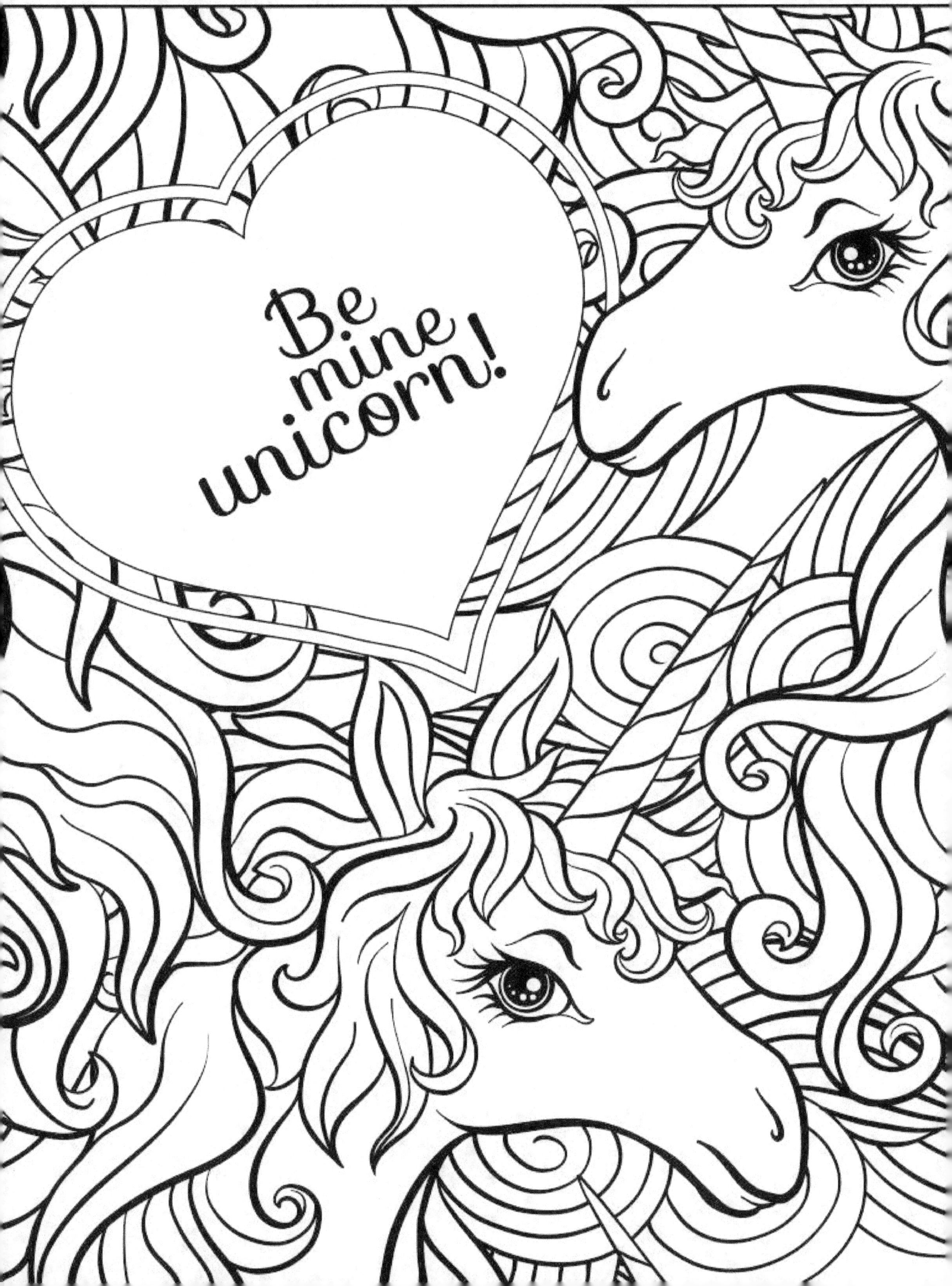
Be mine unicorn!

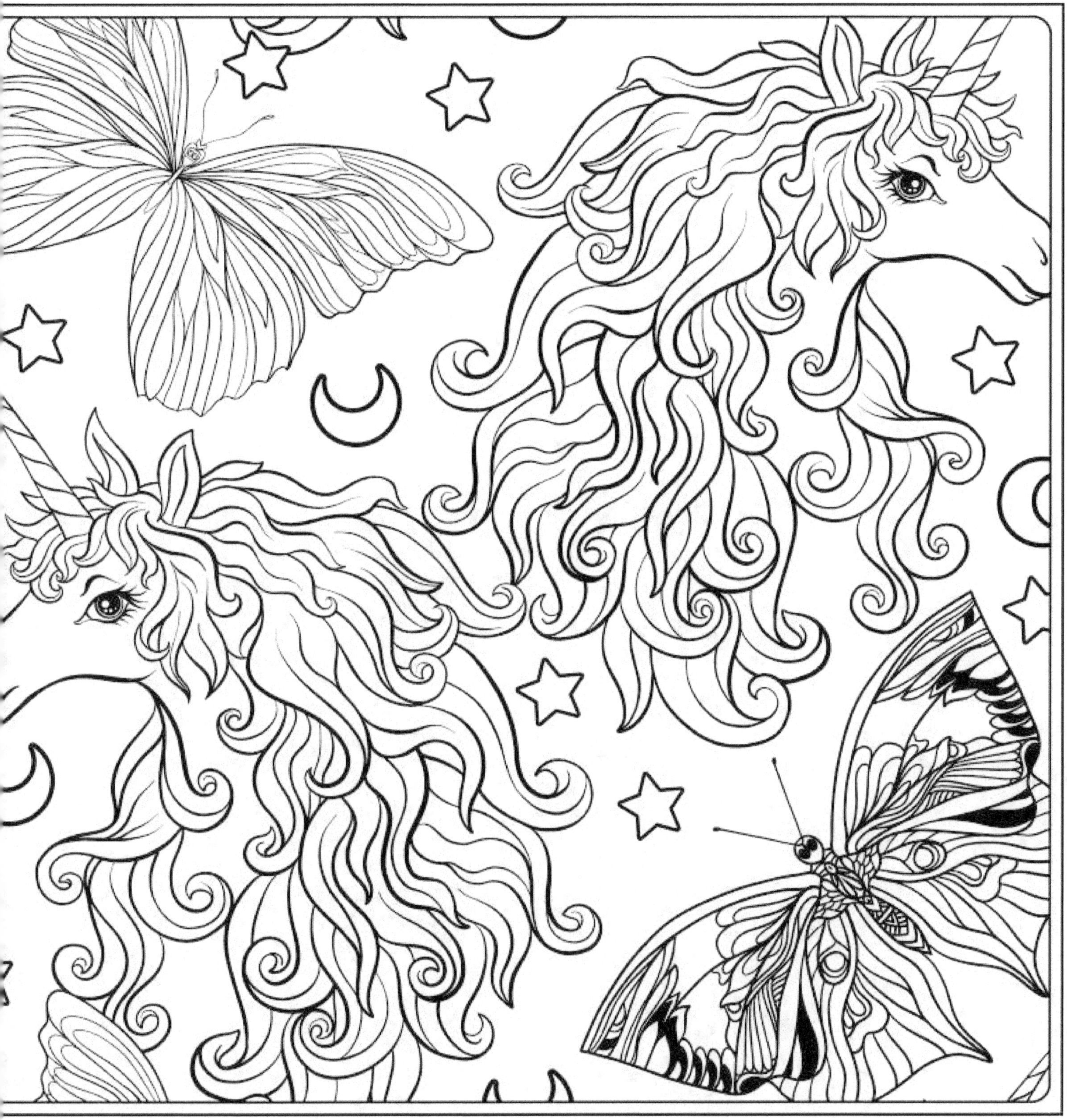

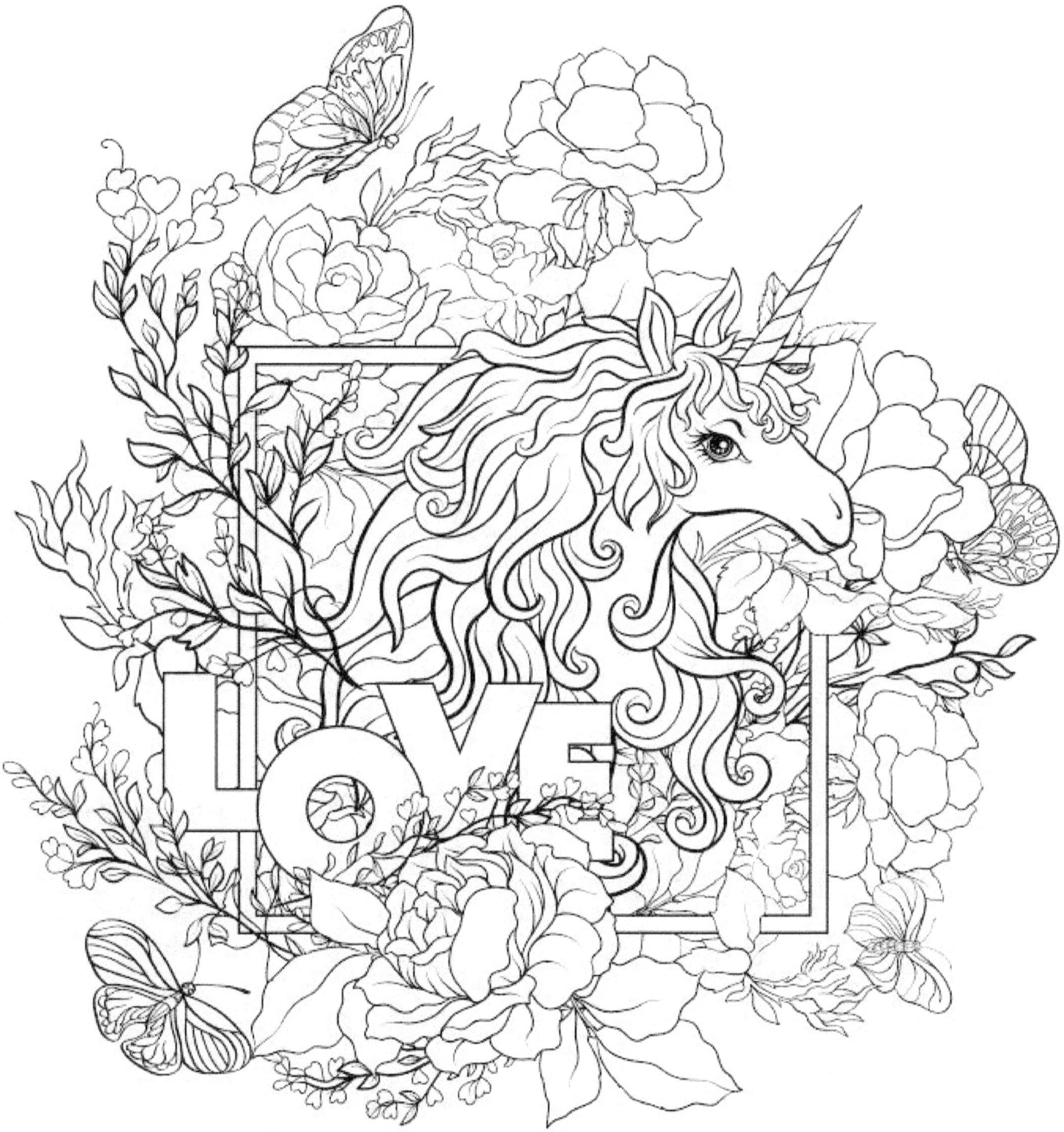
LOVE

Free Surprise Bonus Dolphins Whales Coloring Pages. Enjoy!

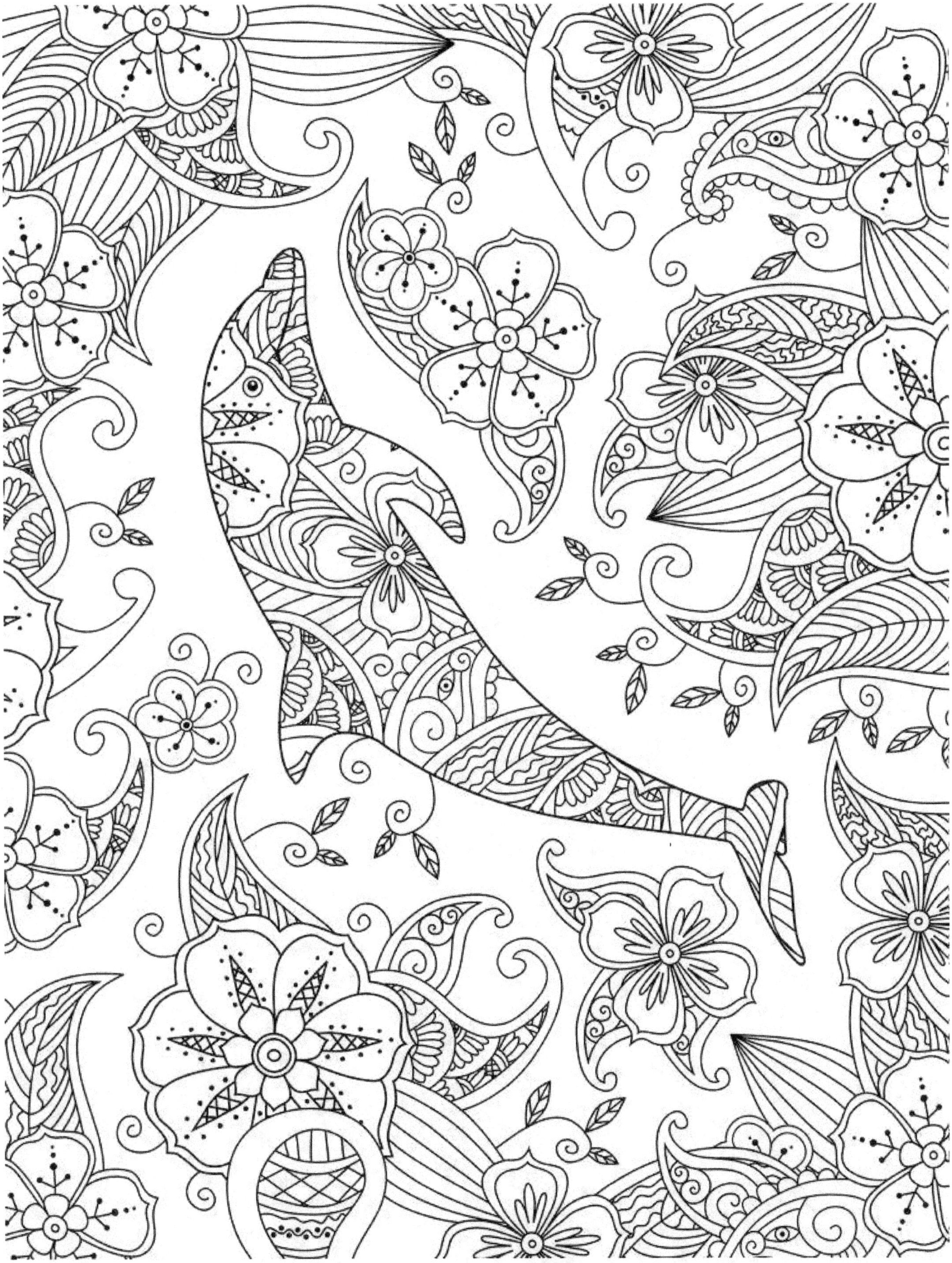

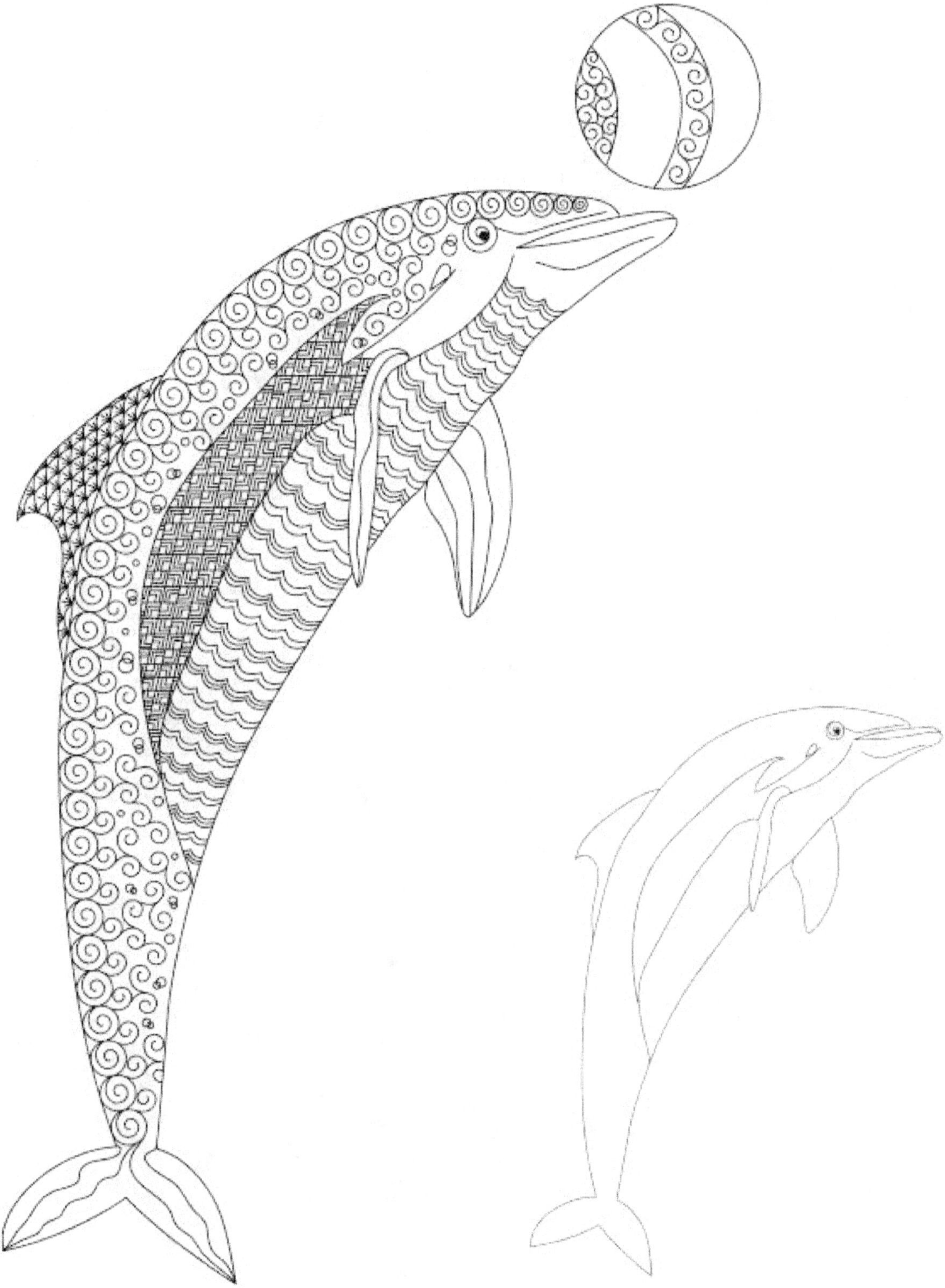

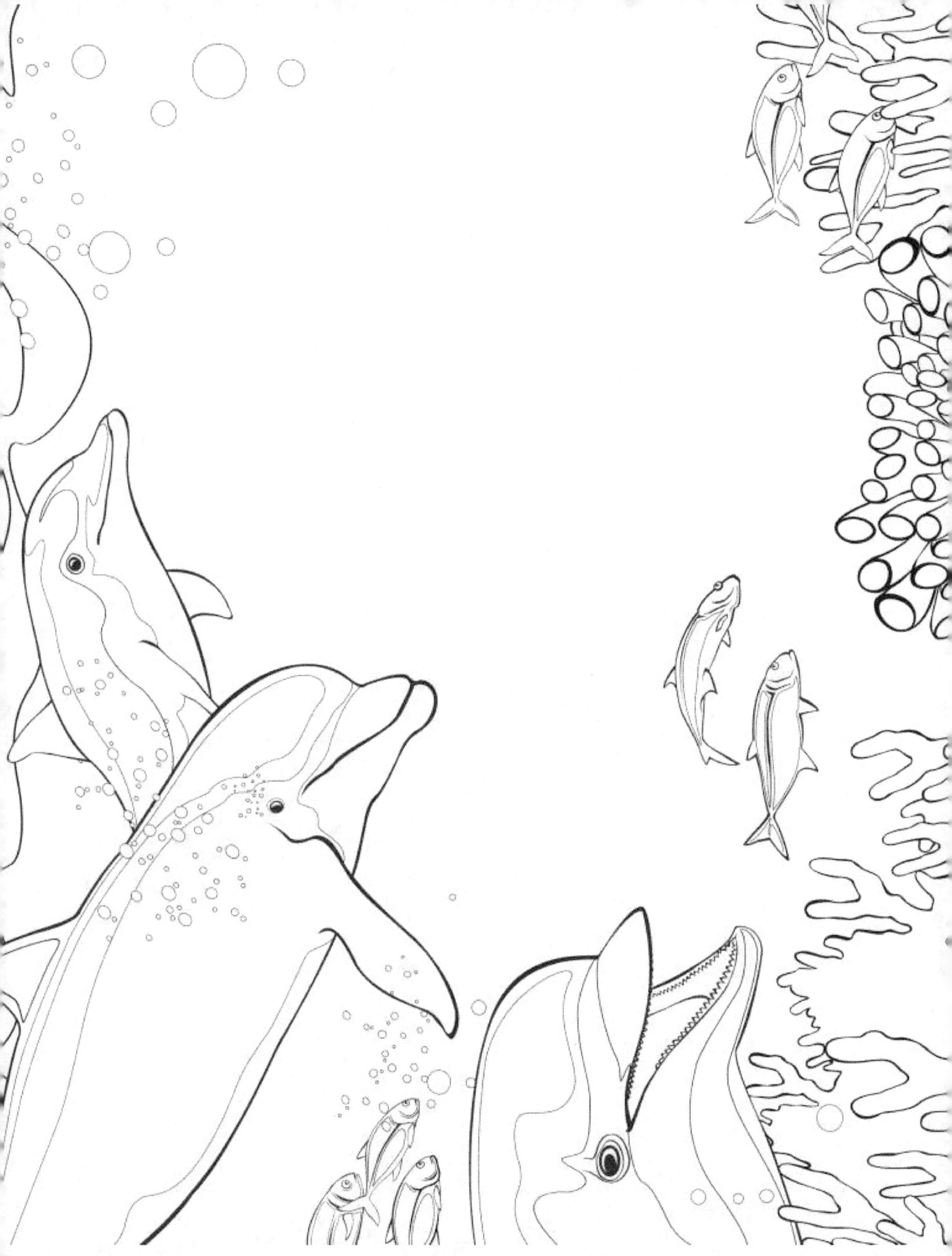

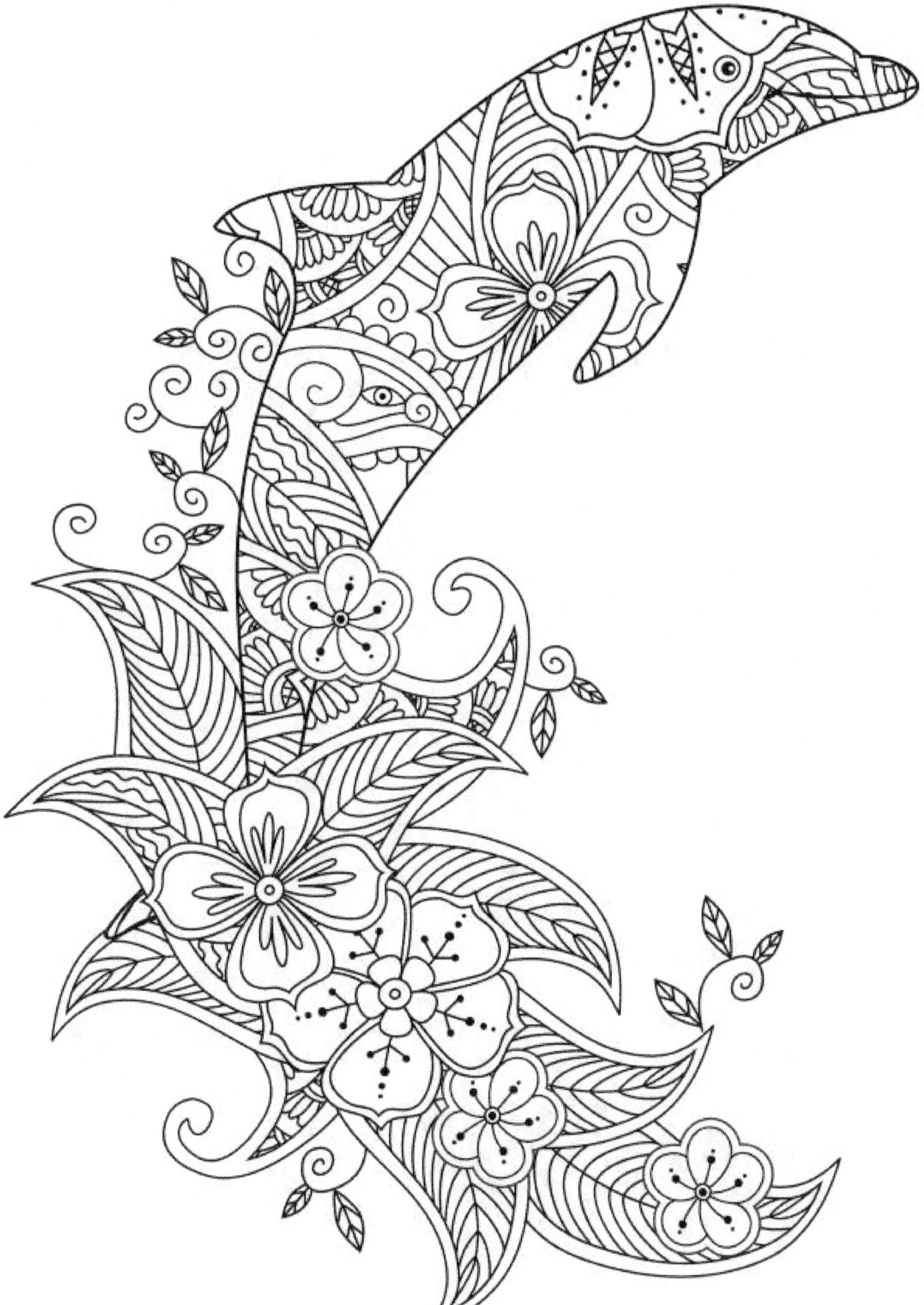

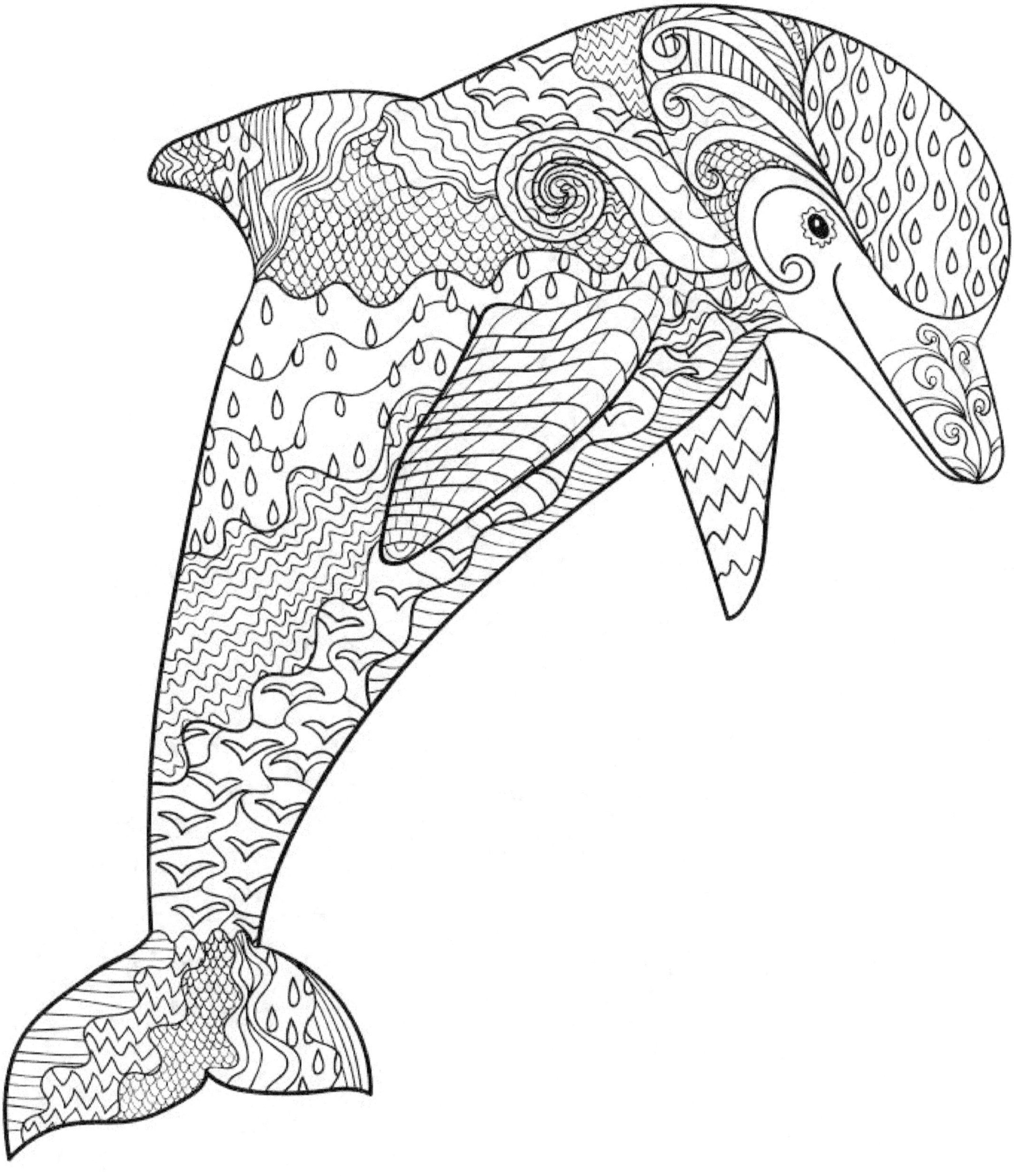

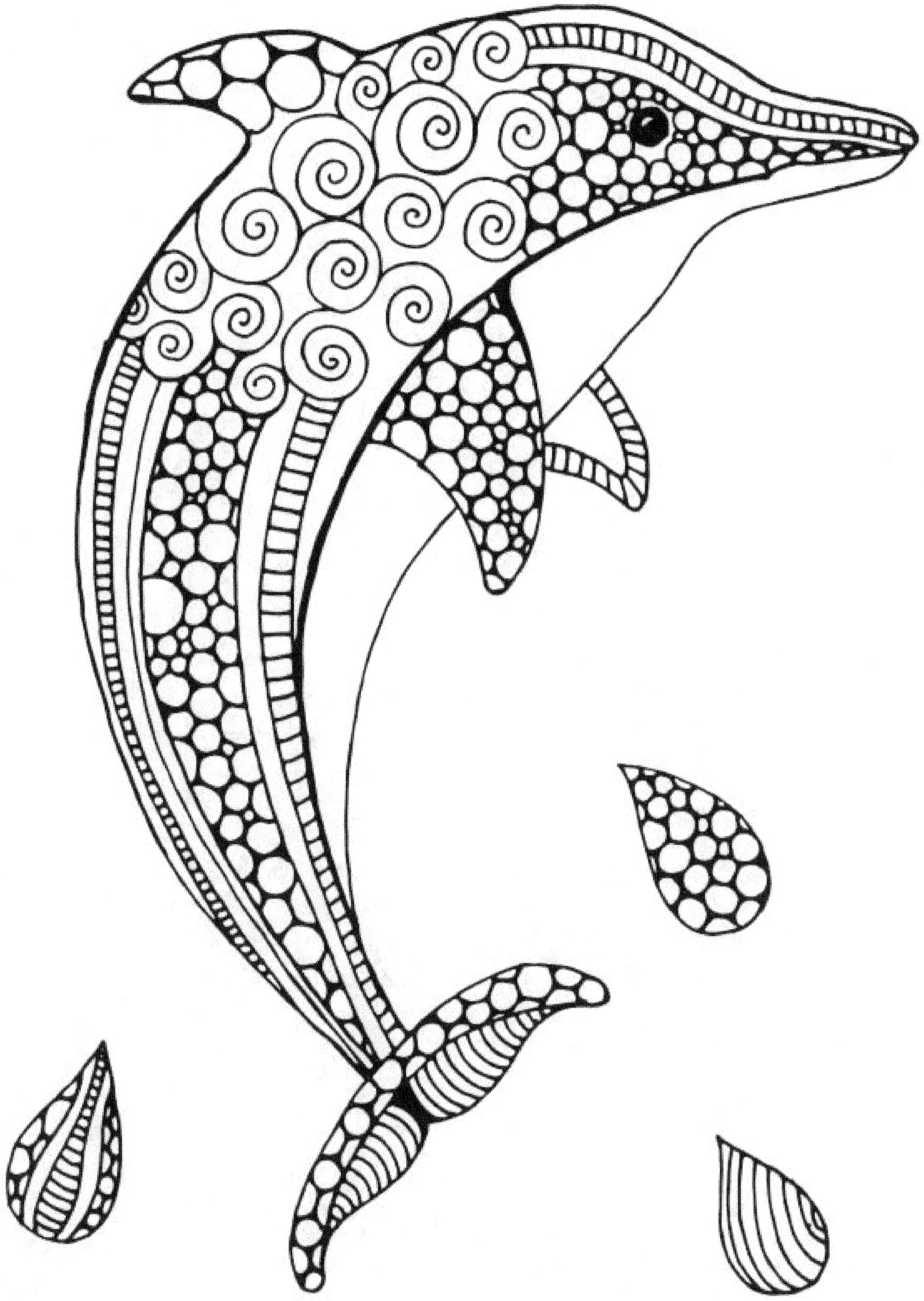

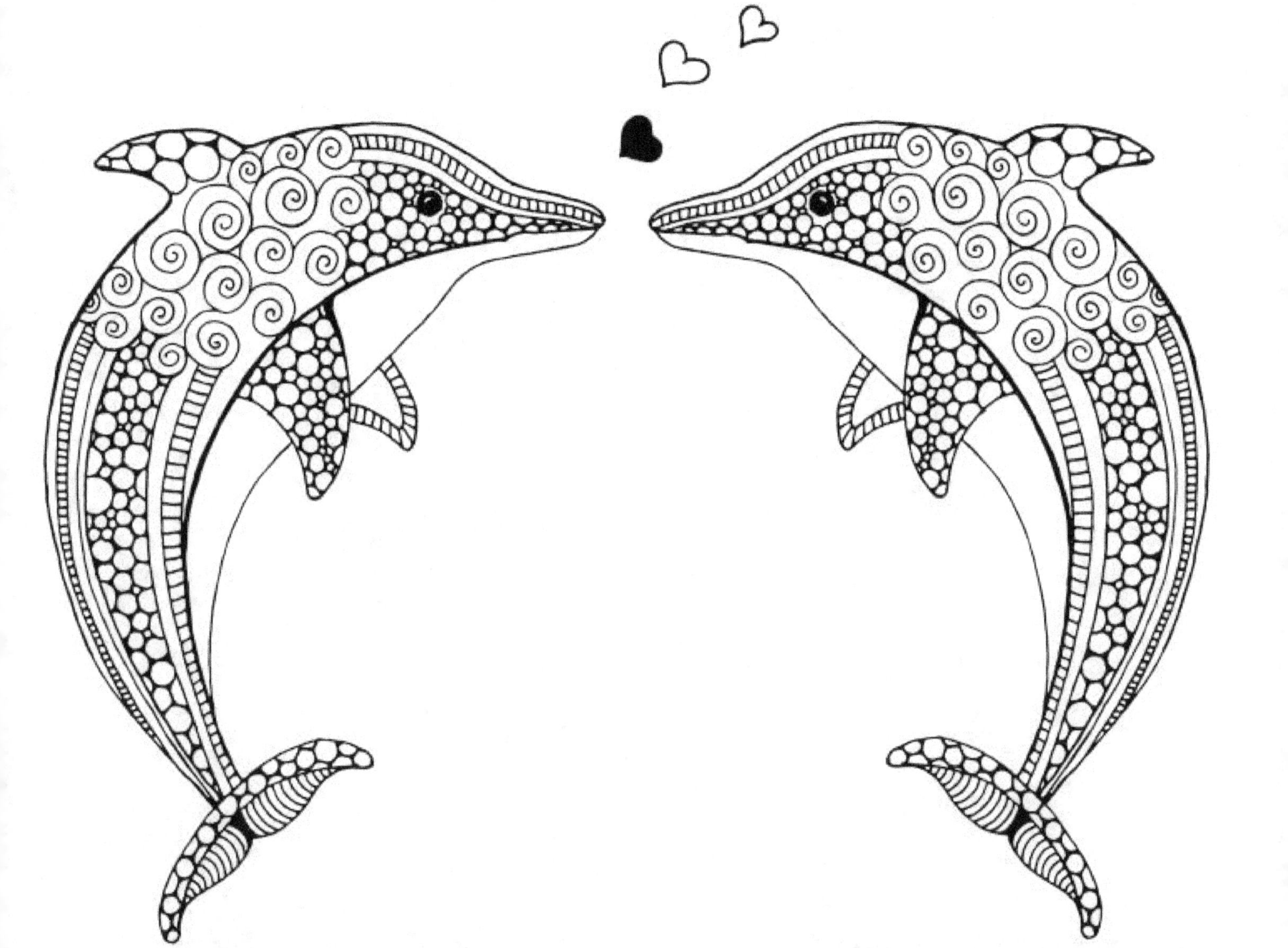

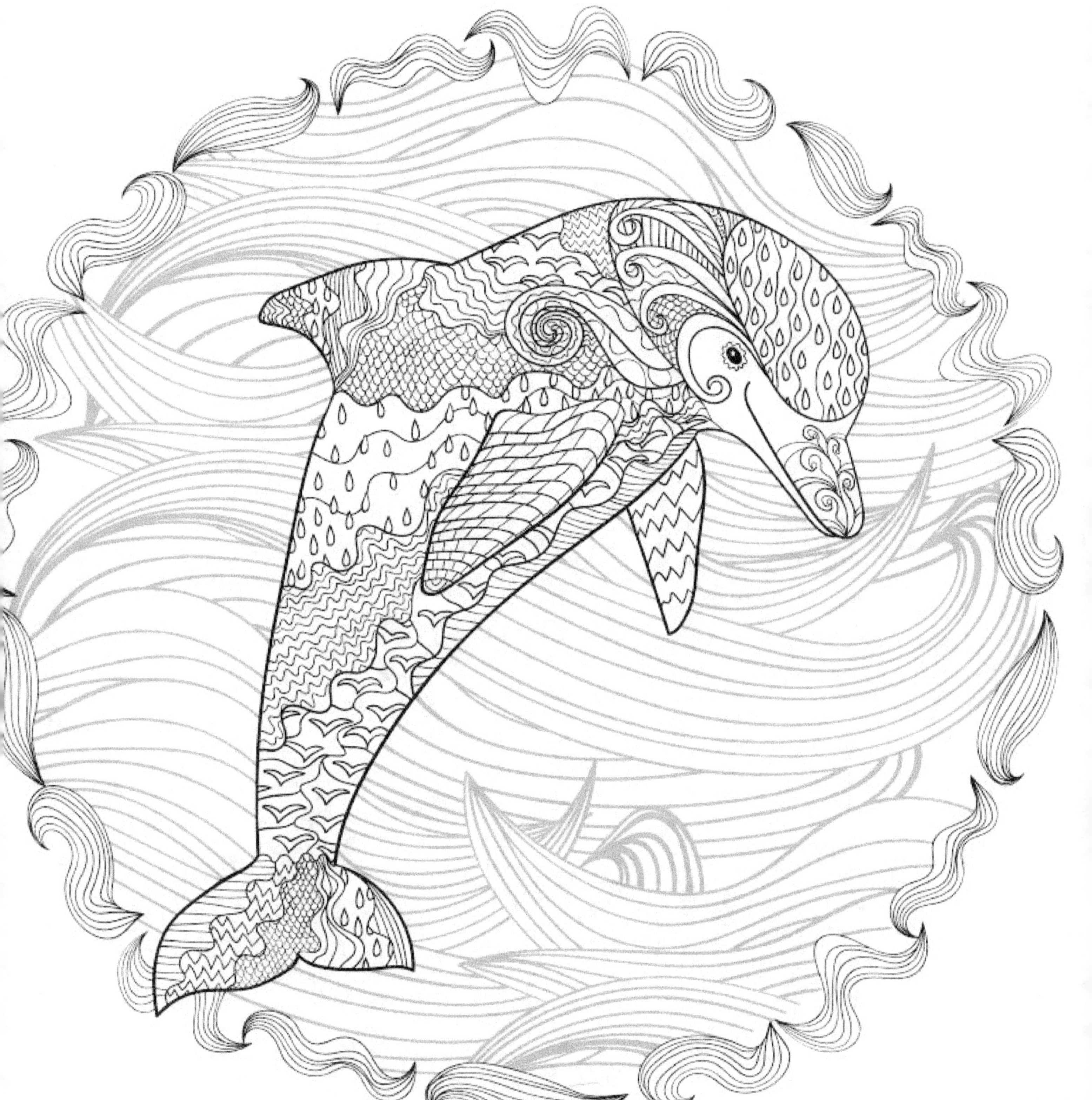

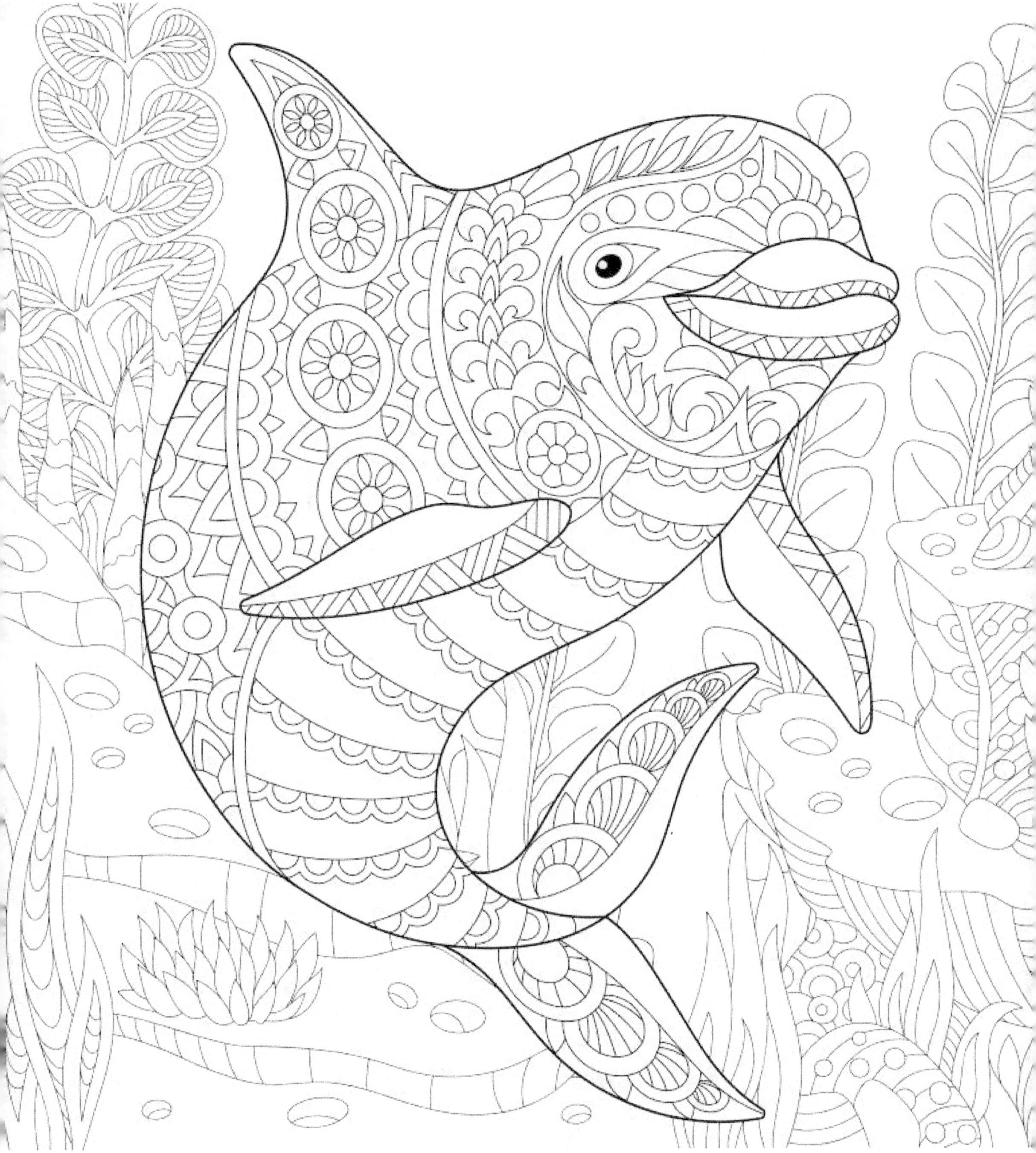

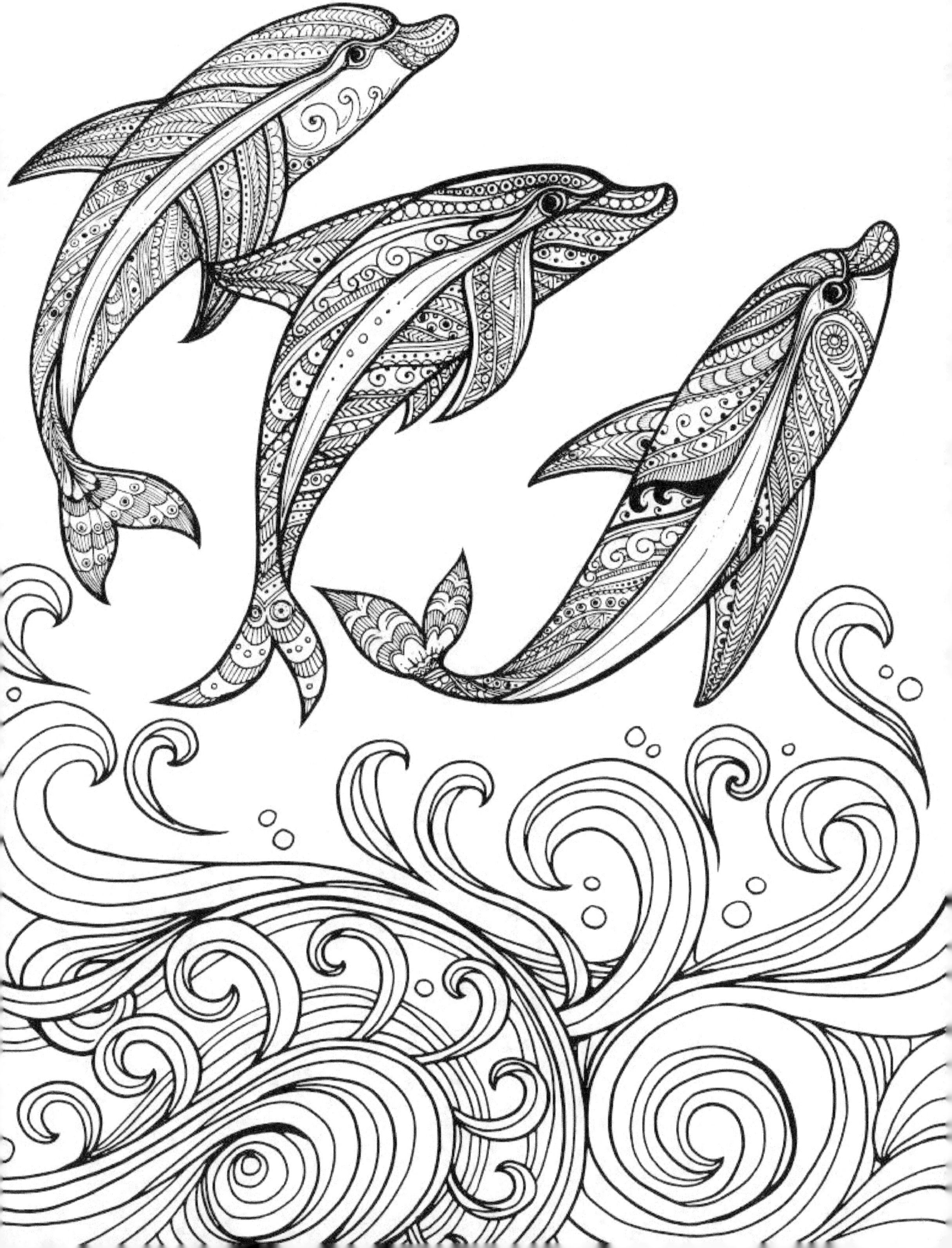

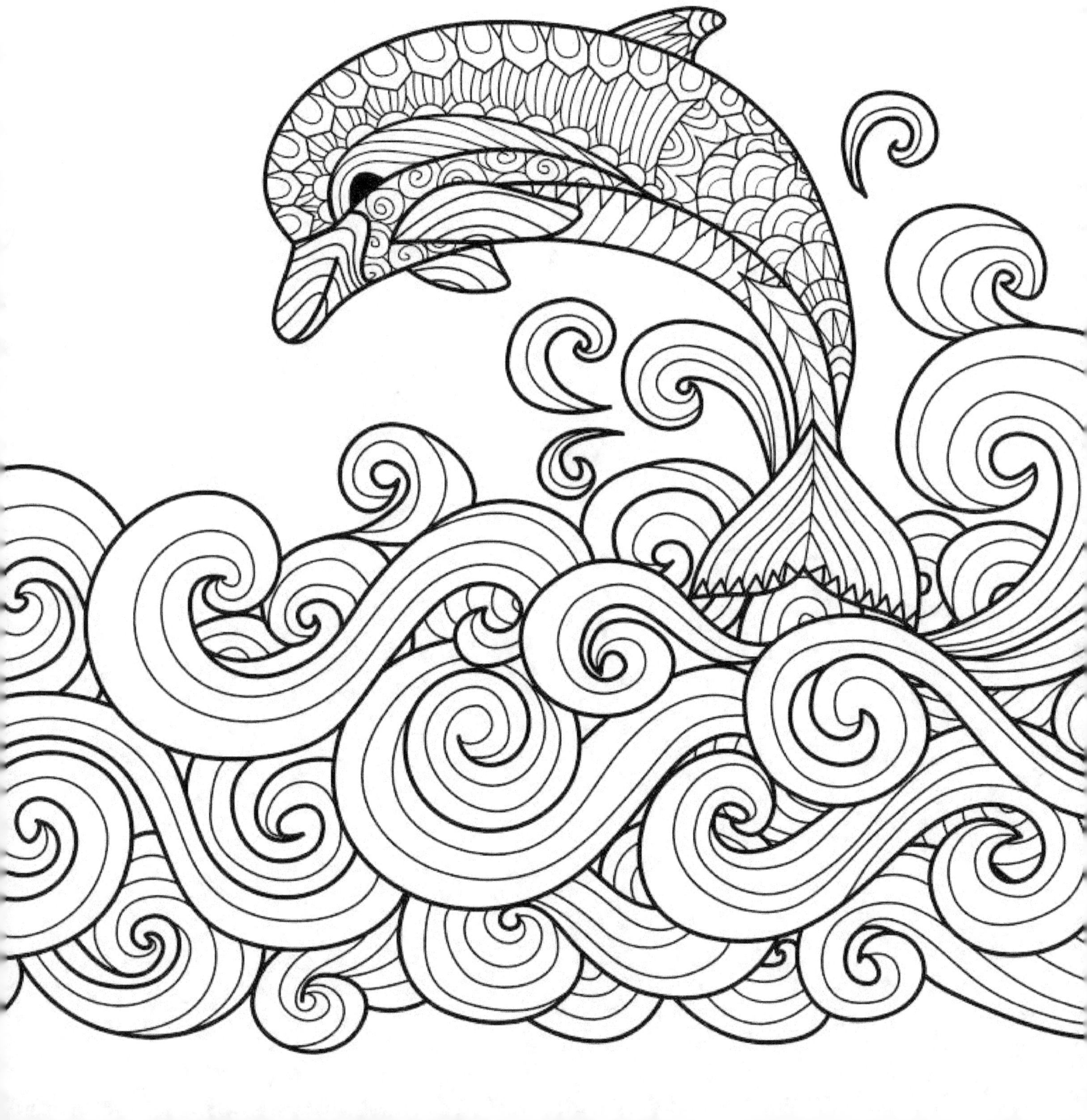

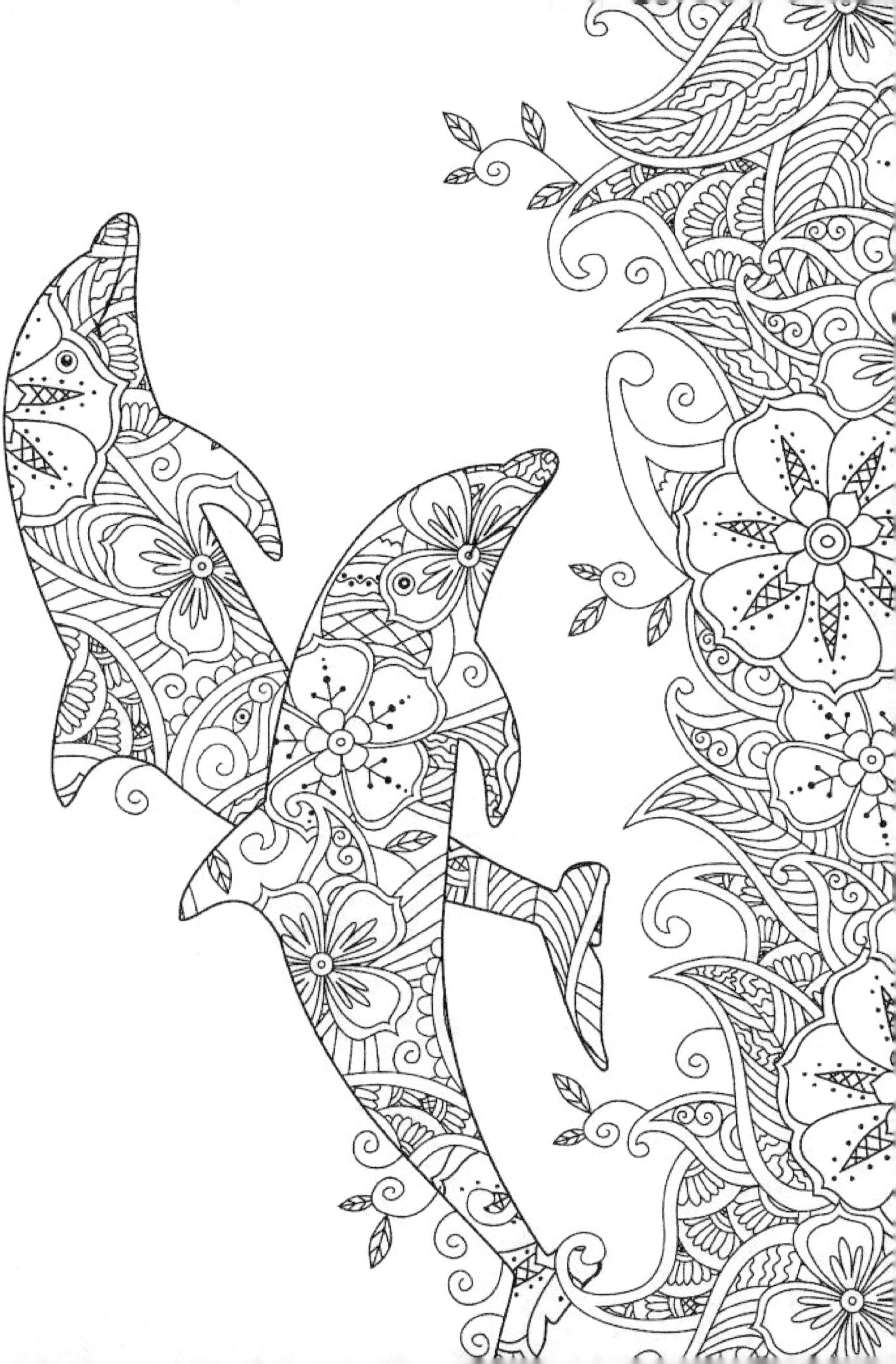

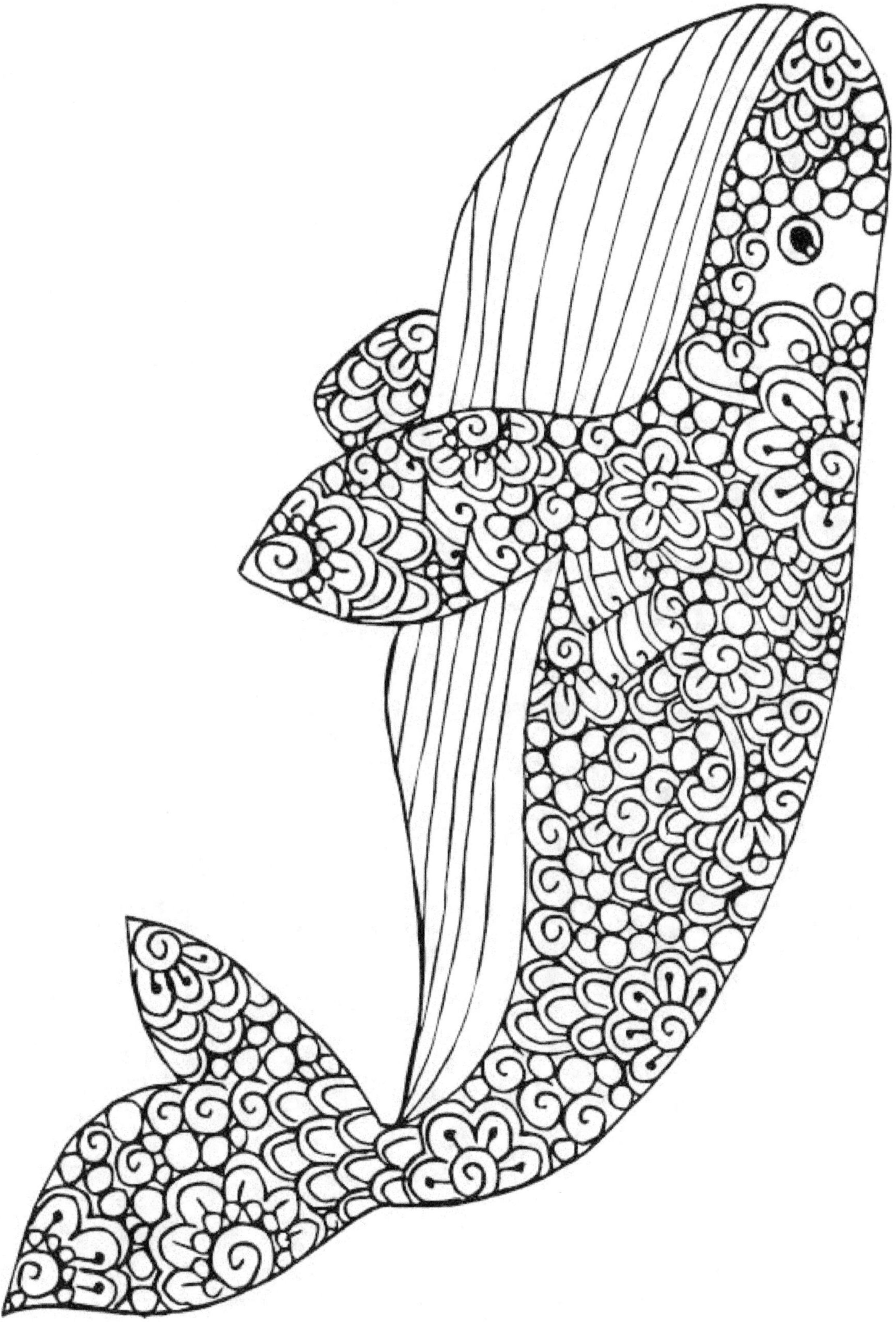

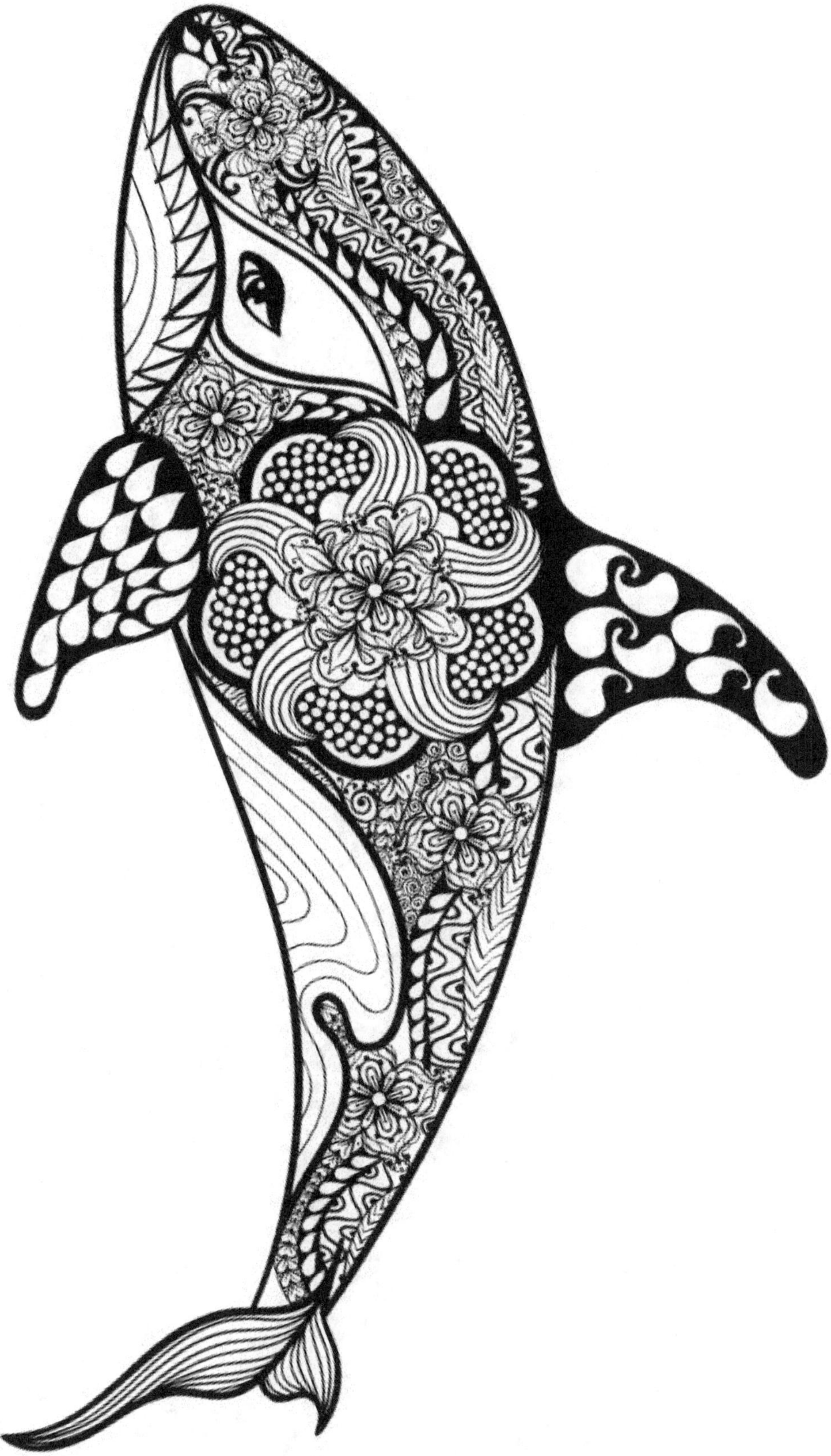

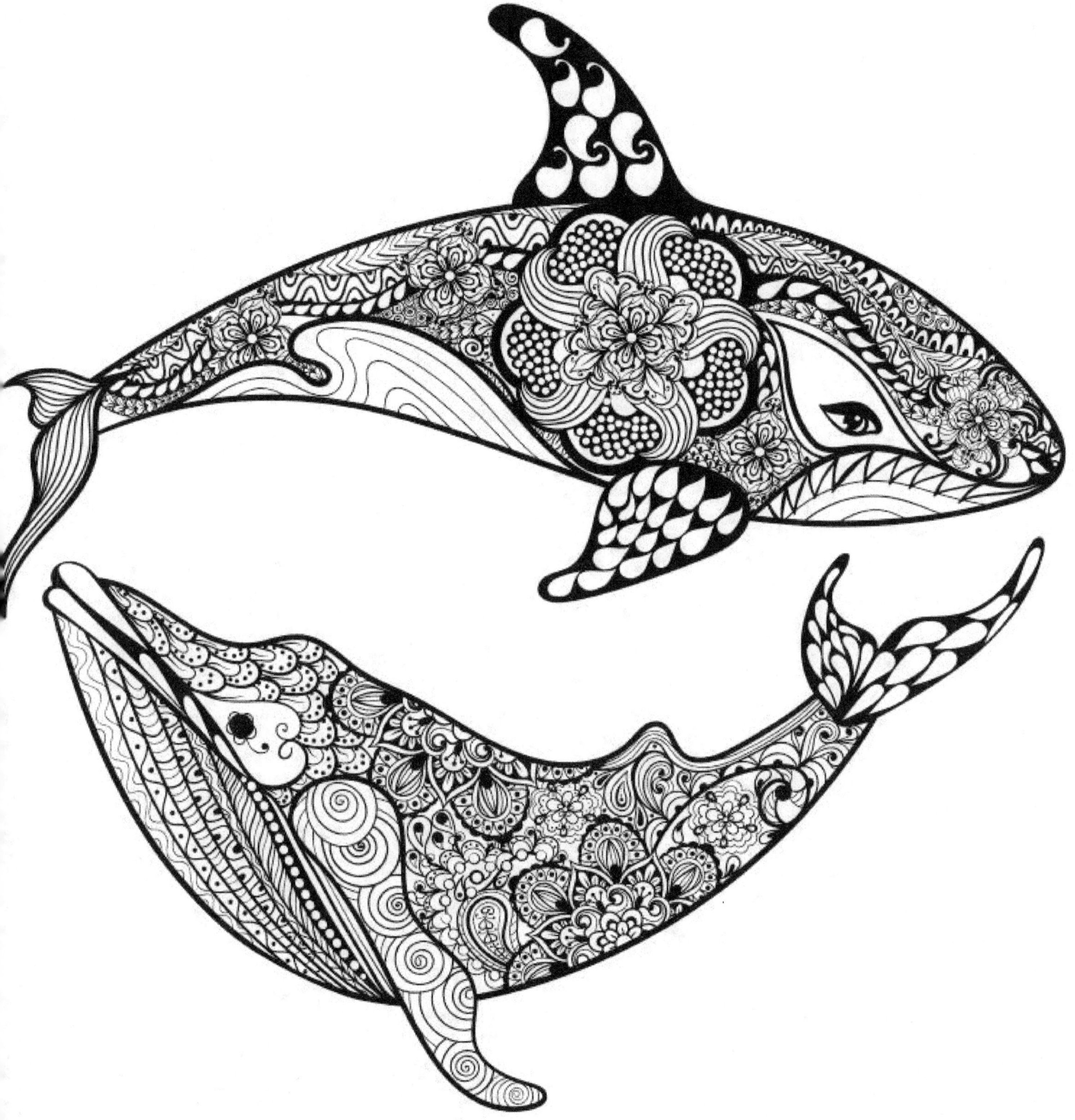

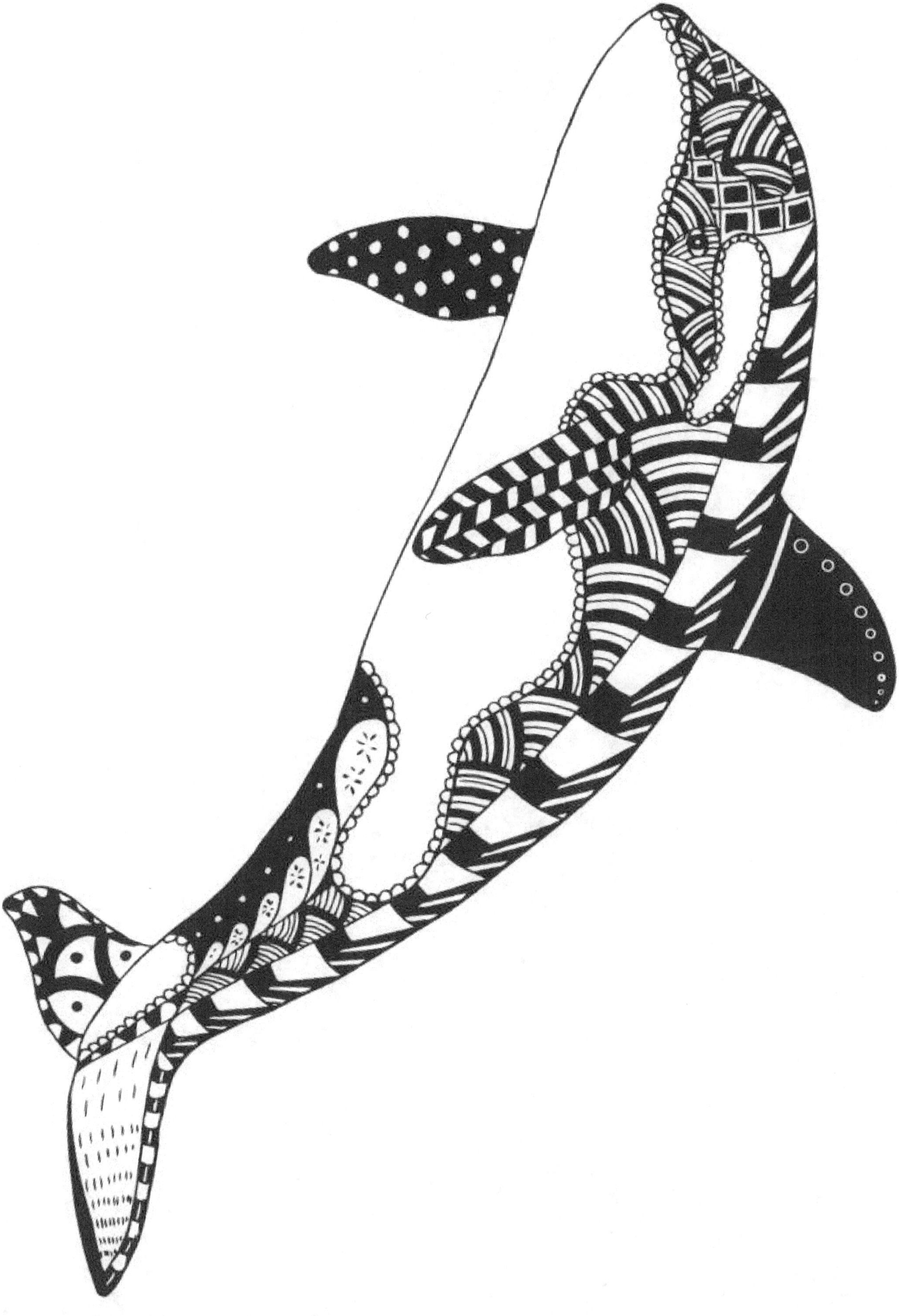

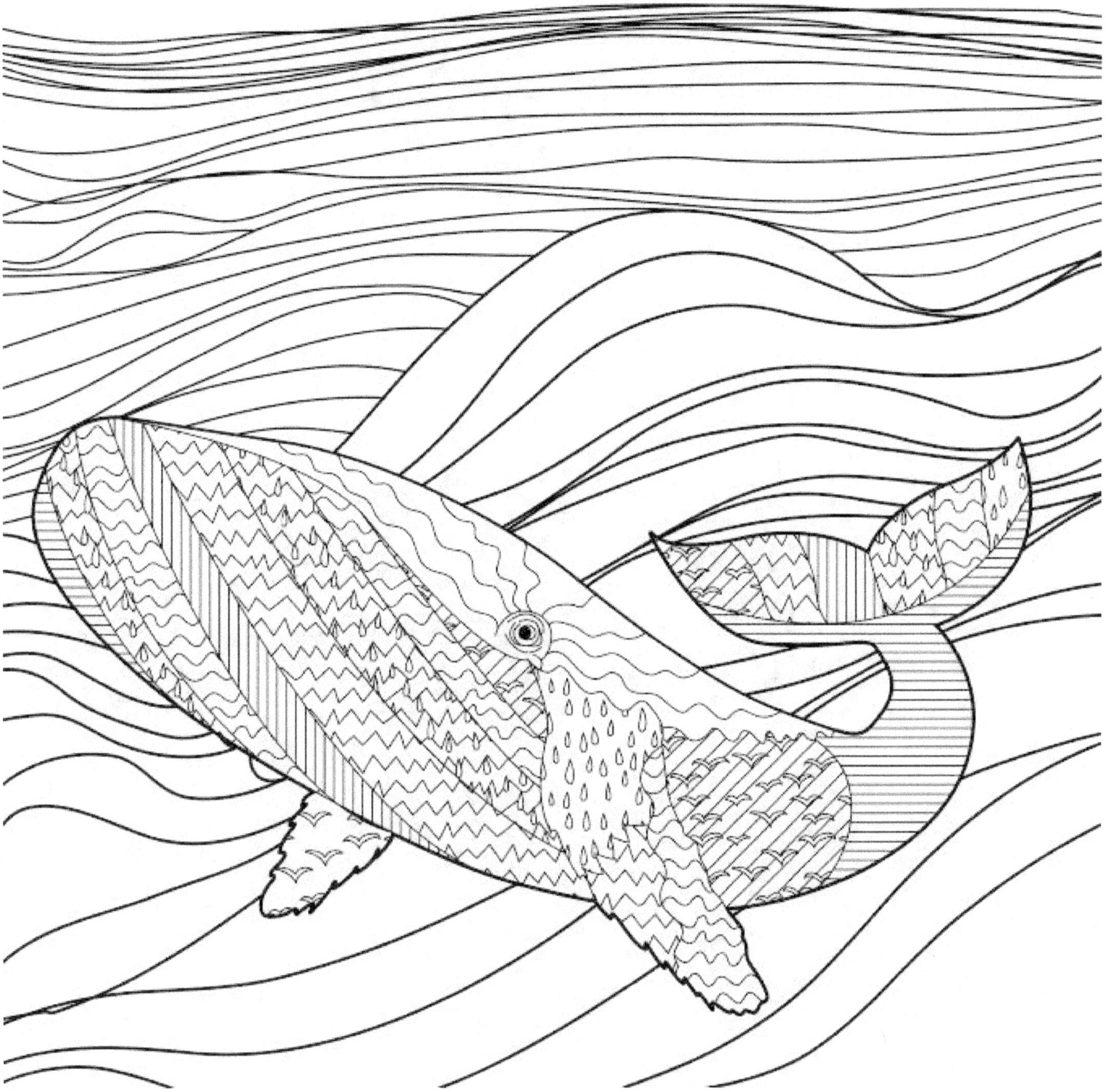

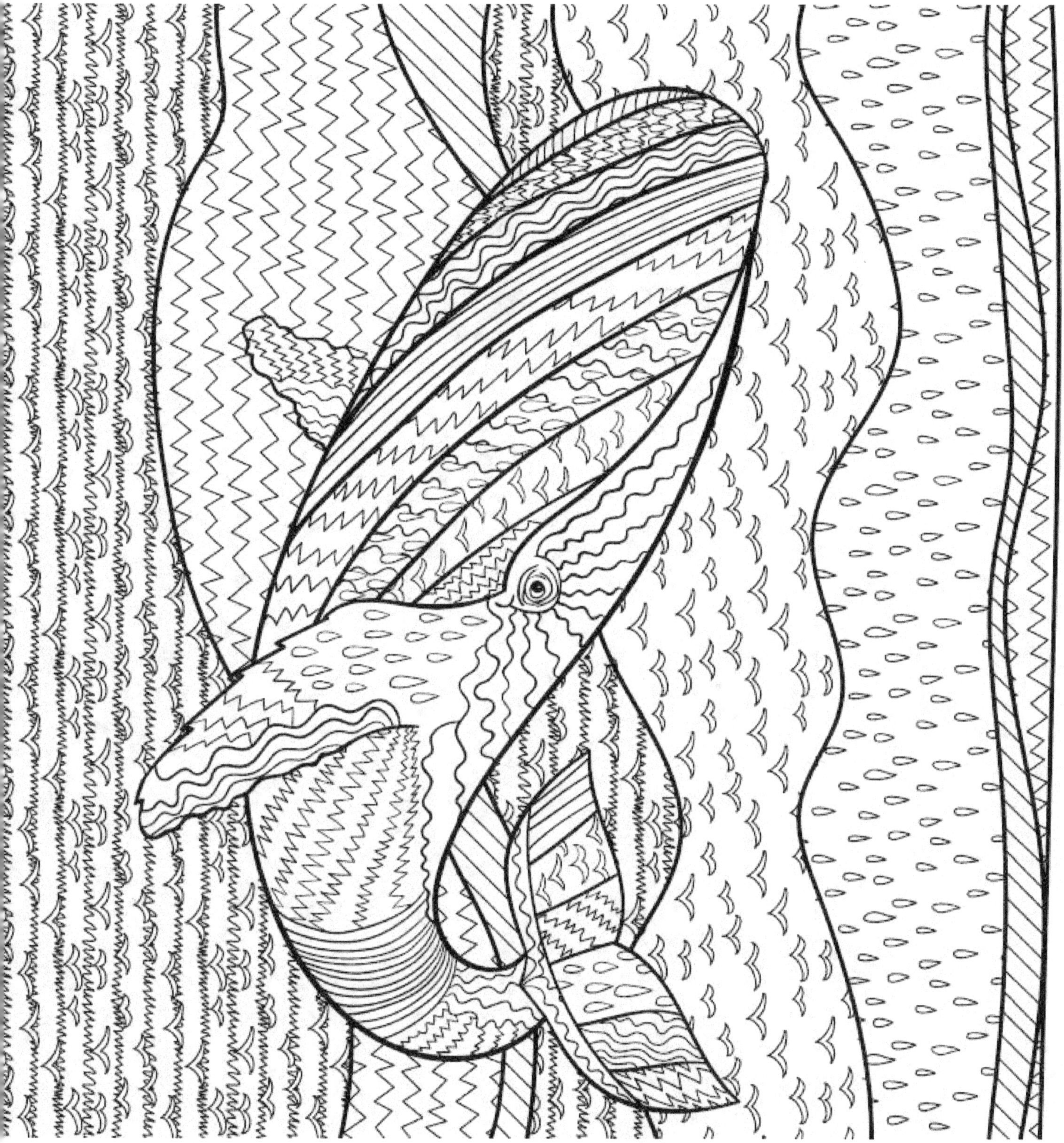

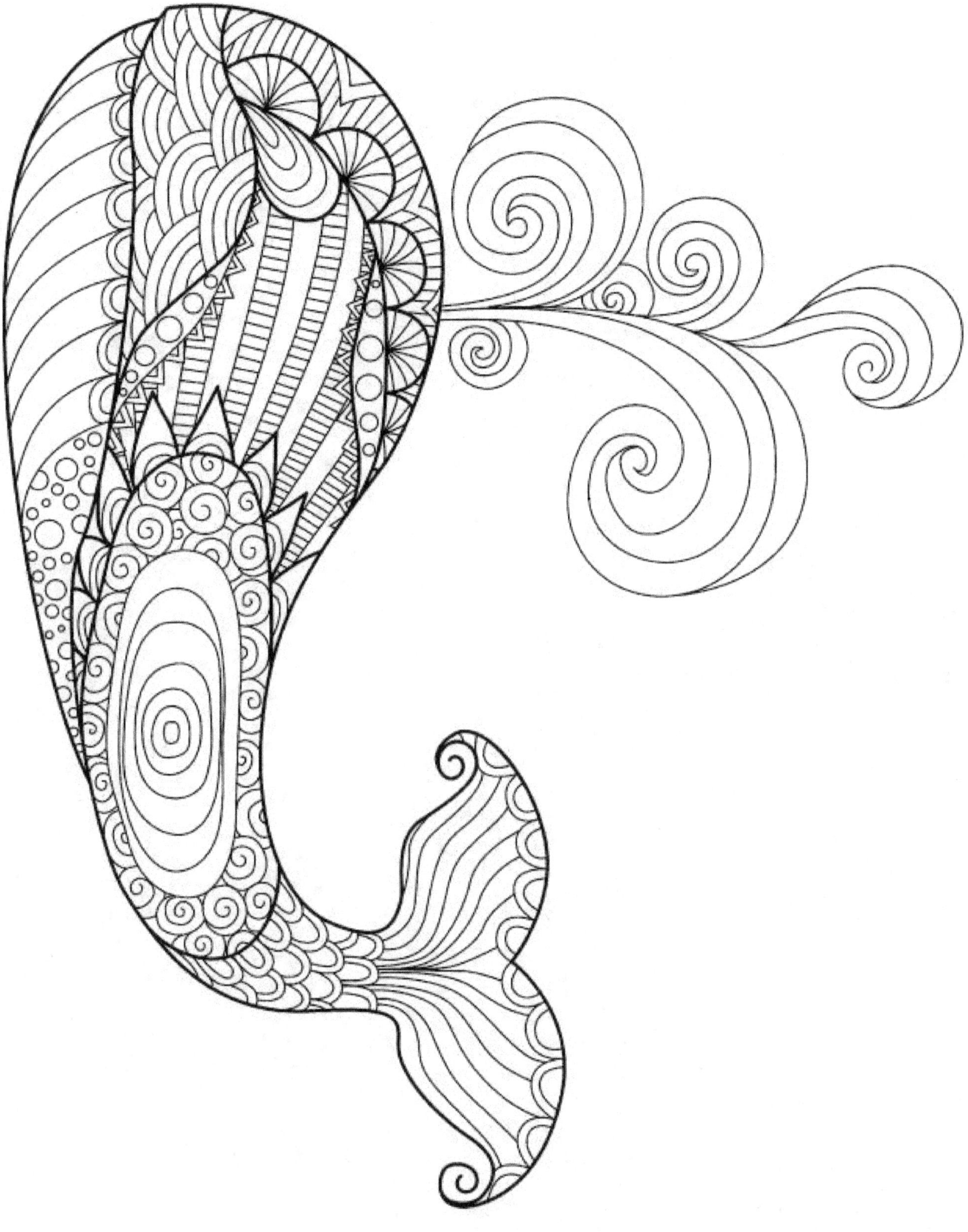

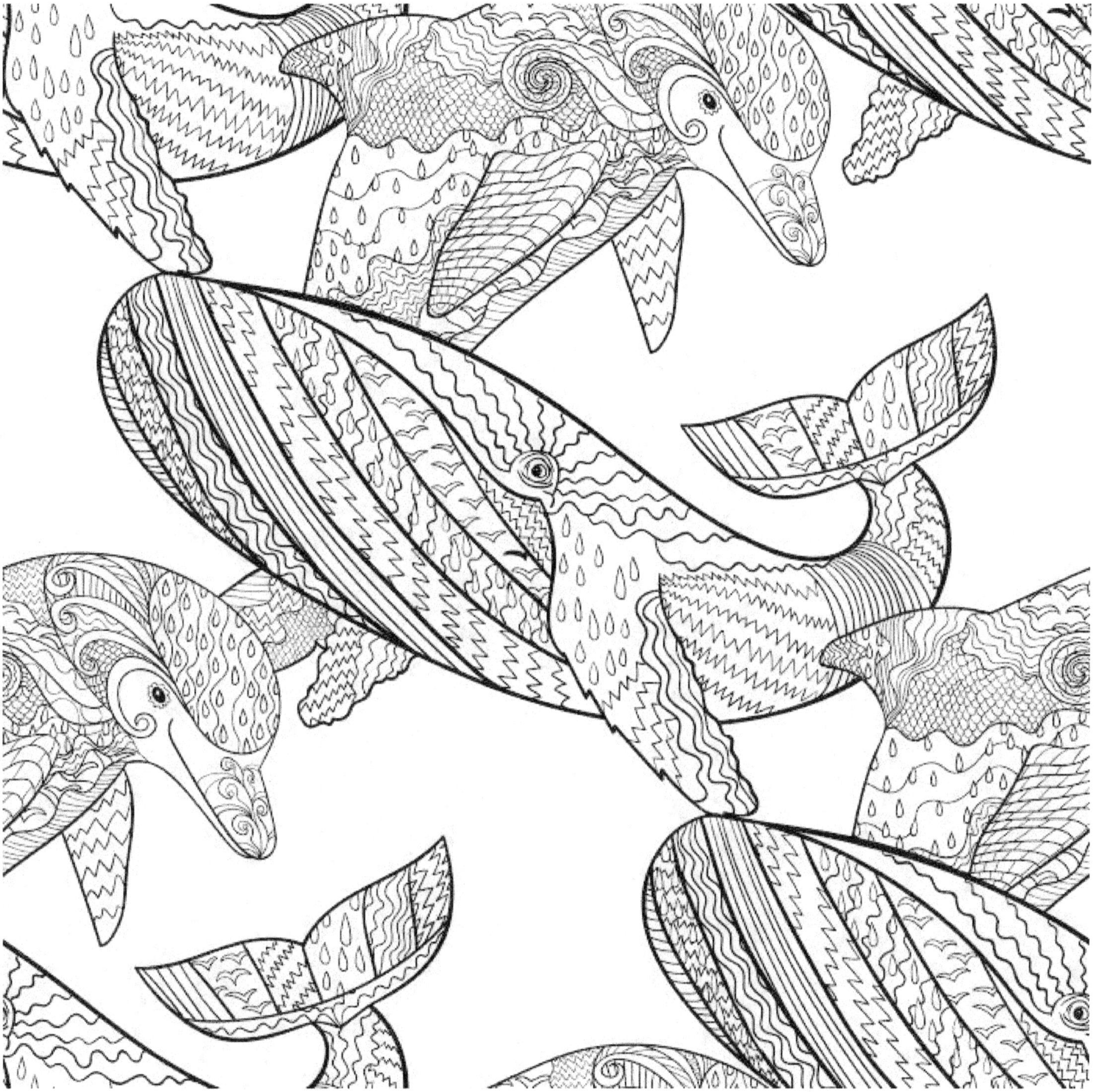

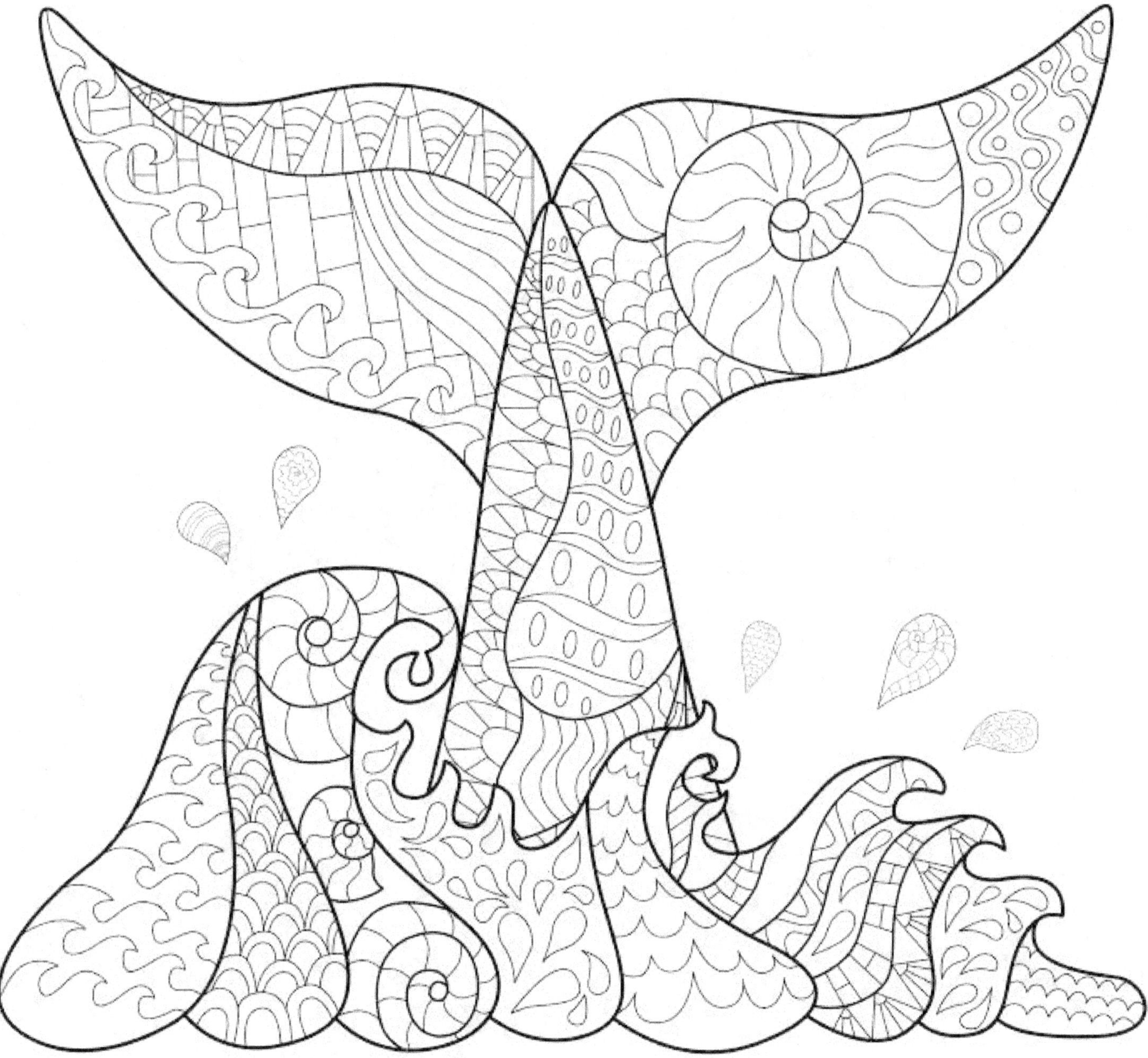

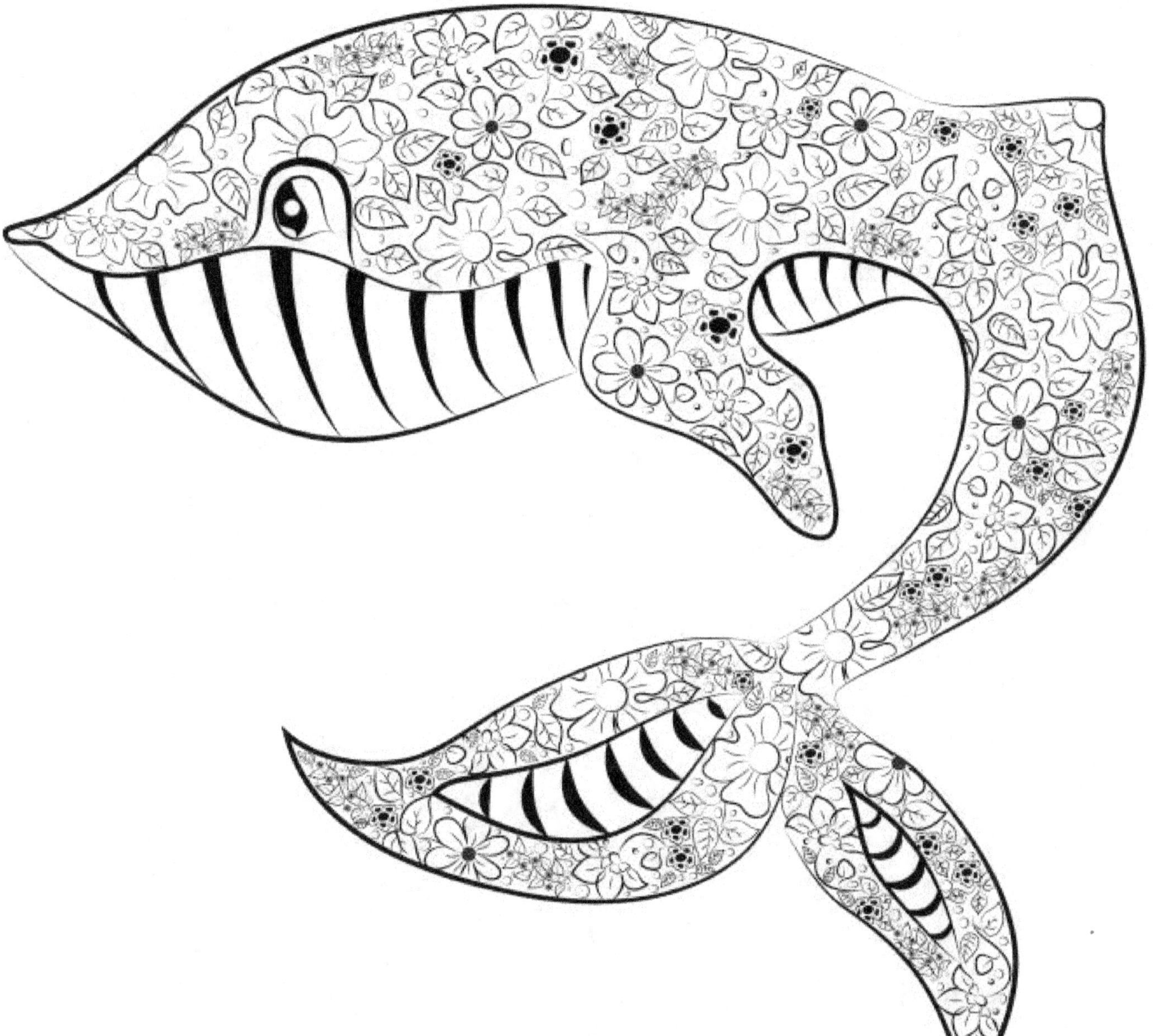

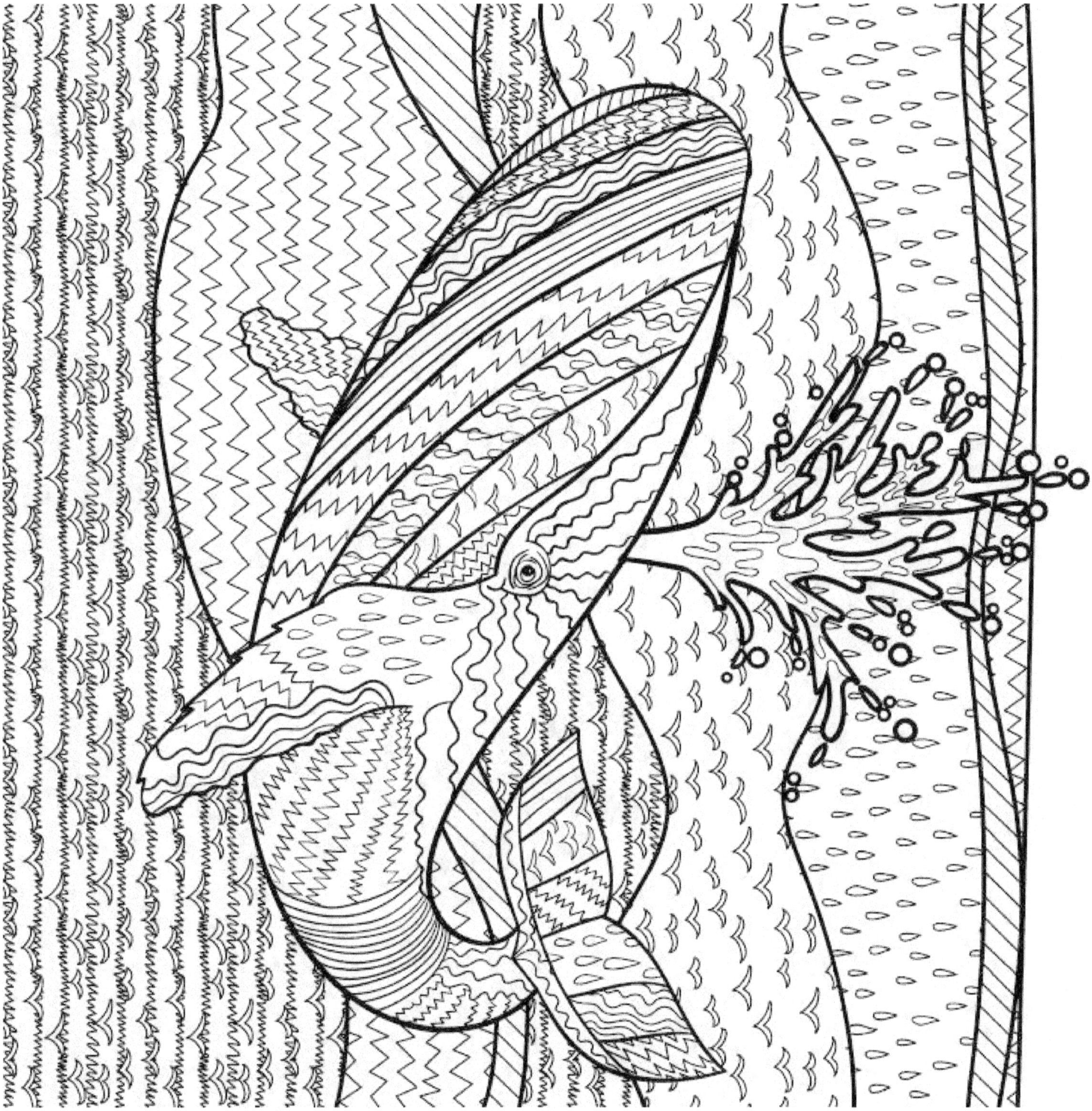

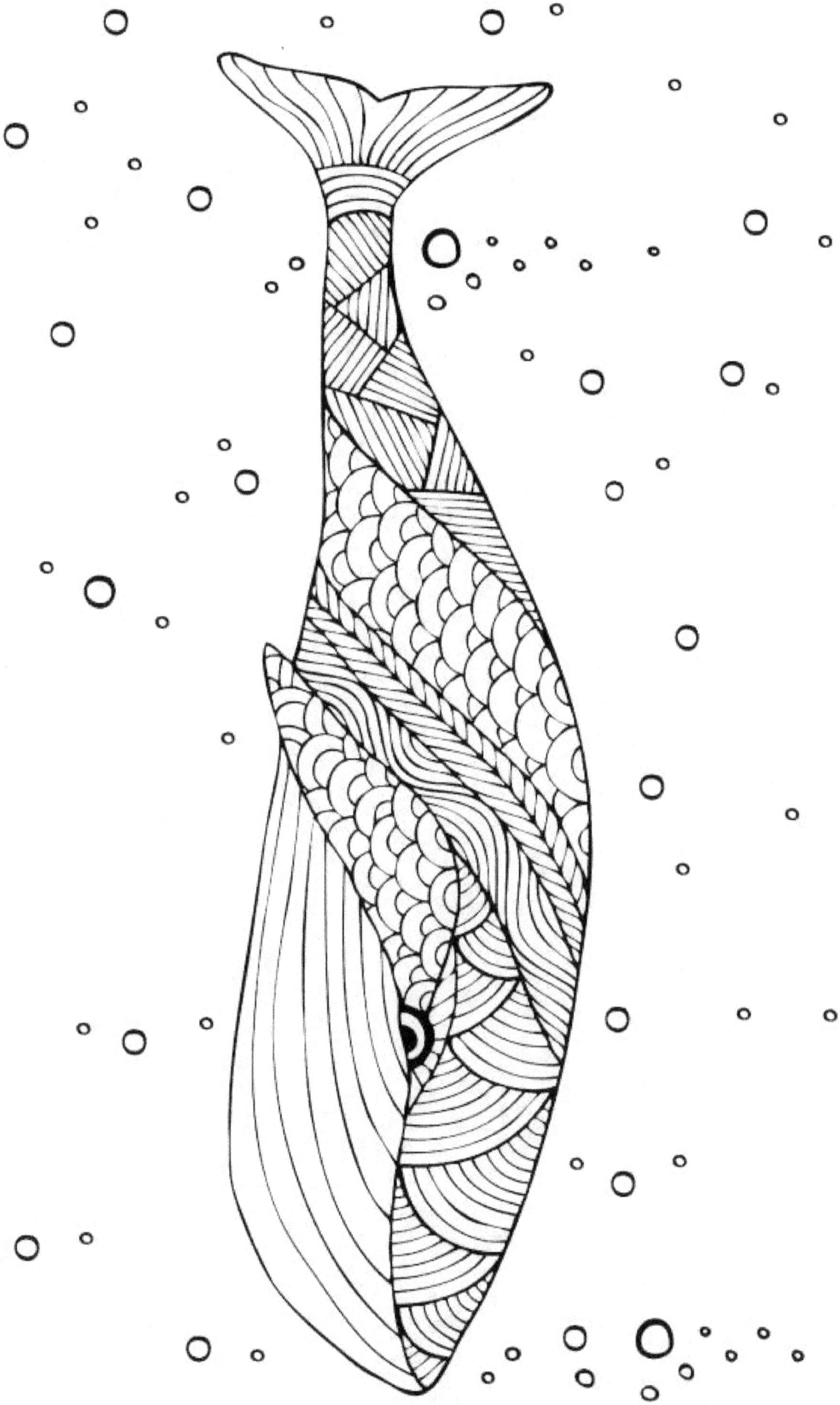

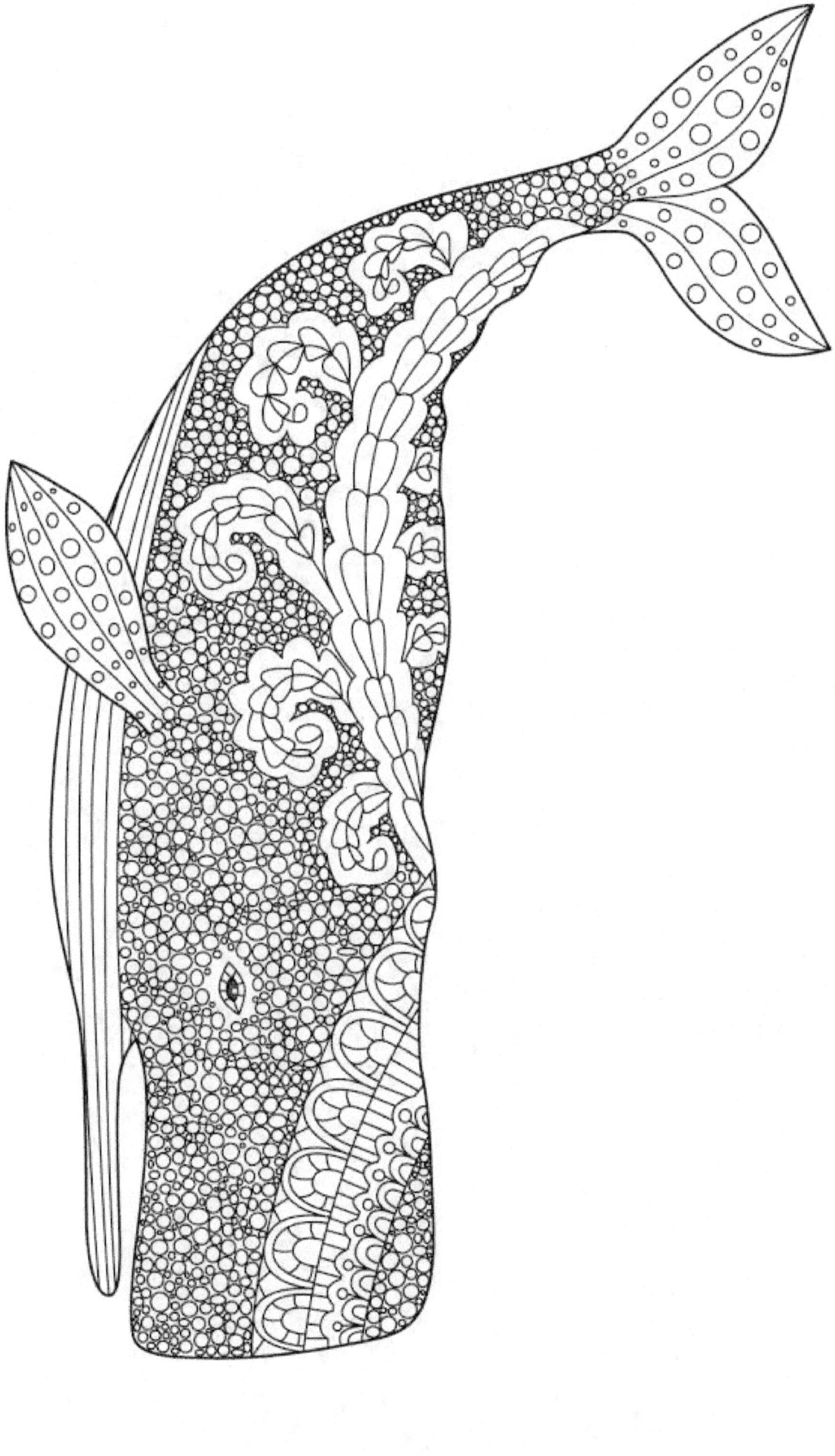

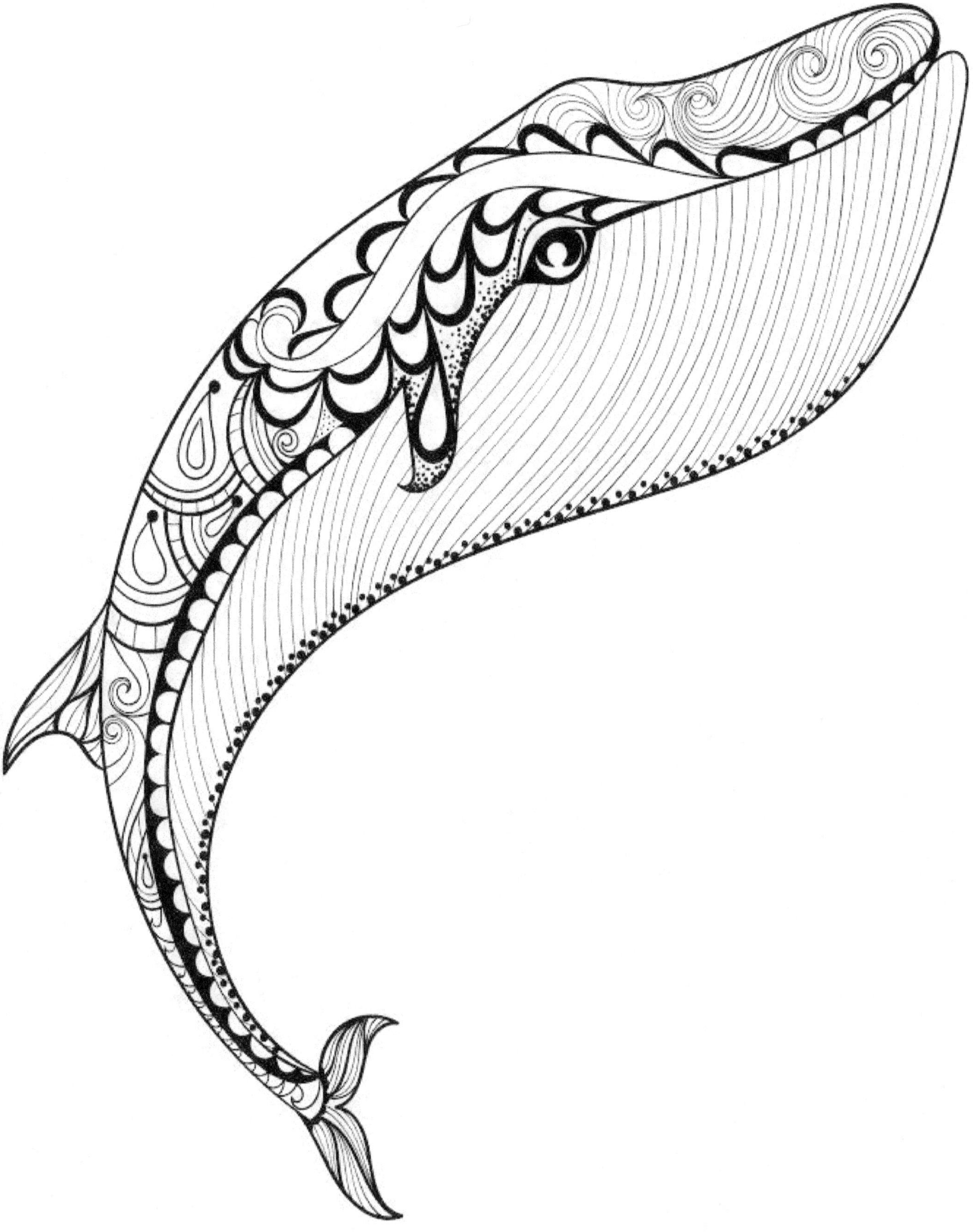

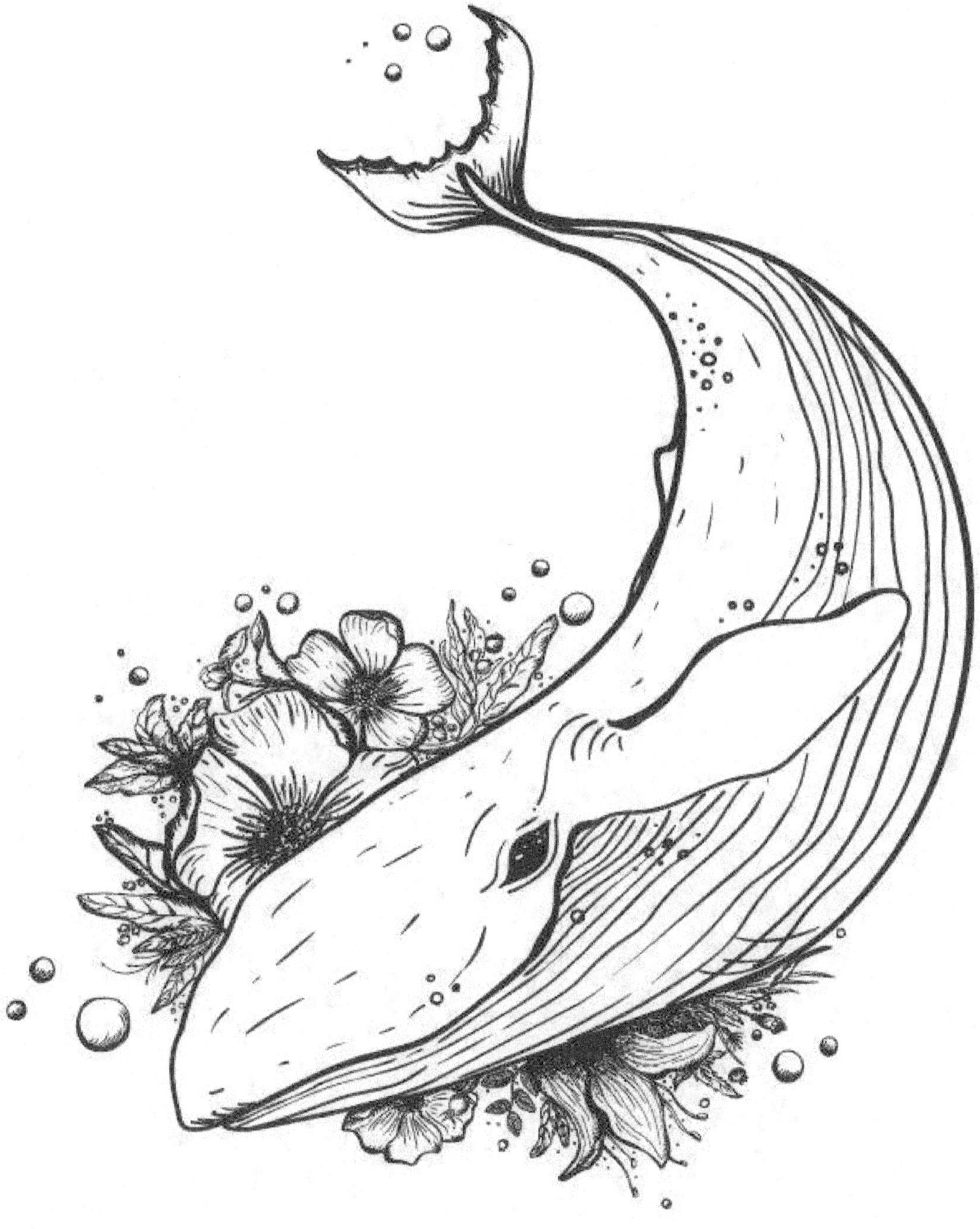

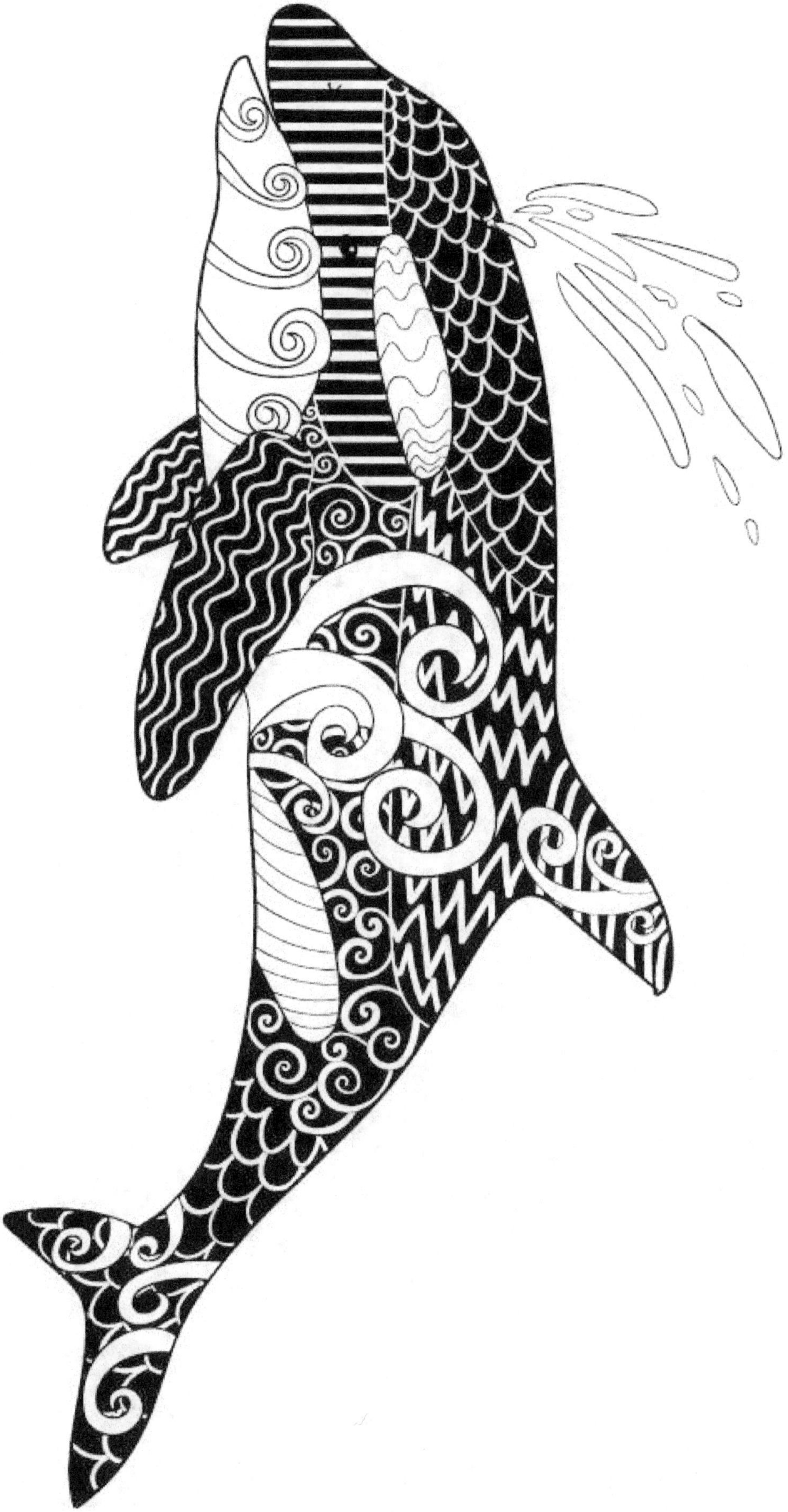

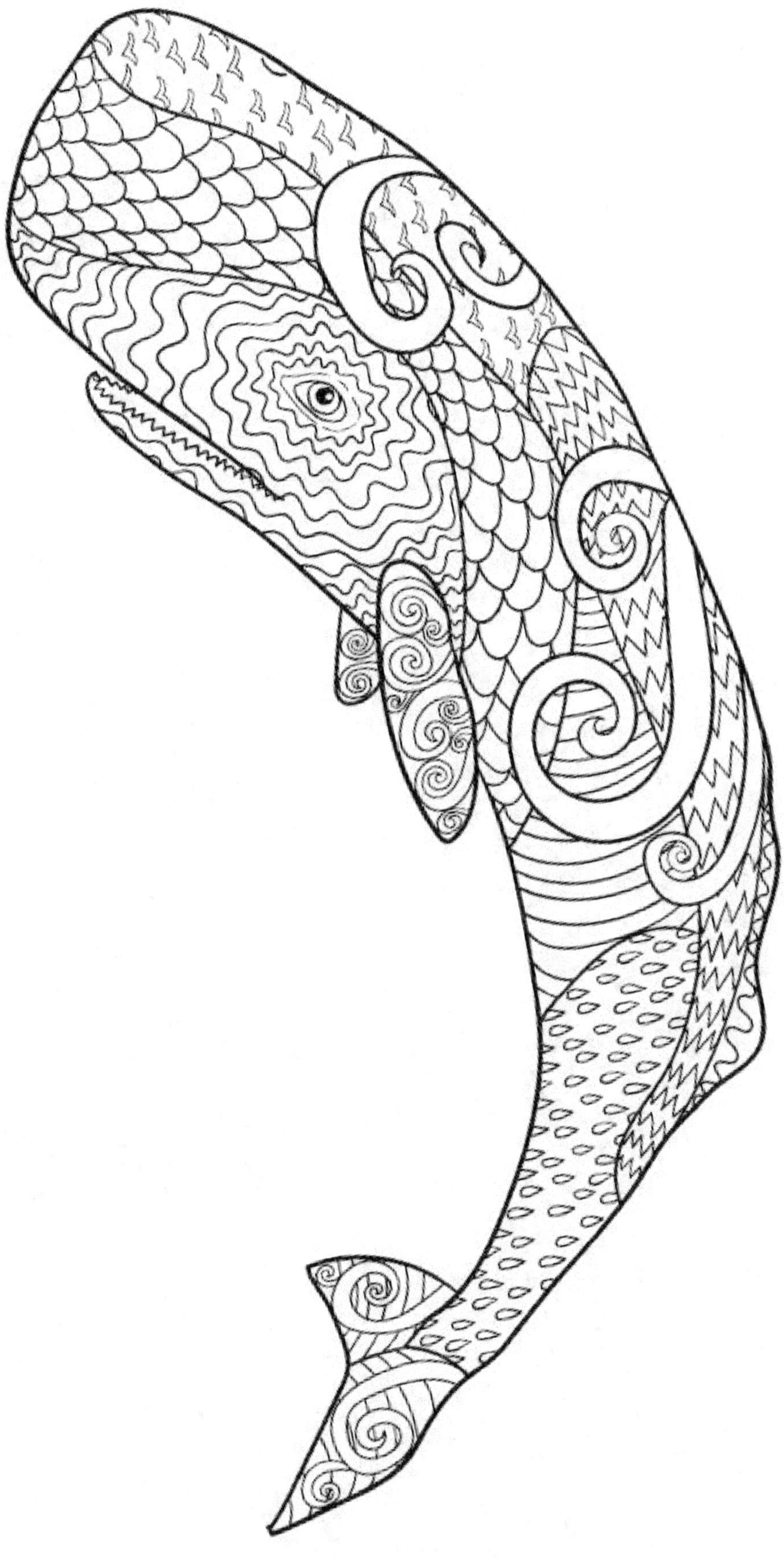

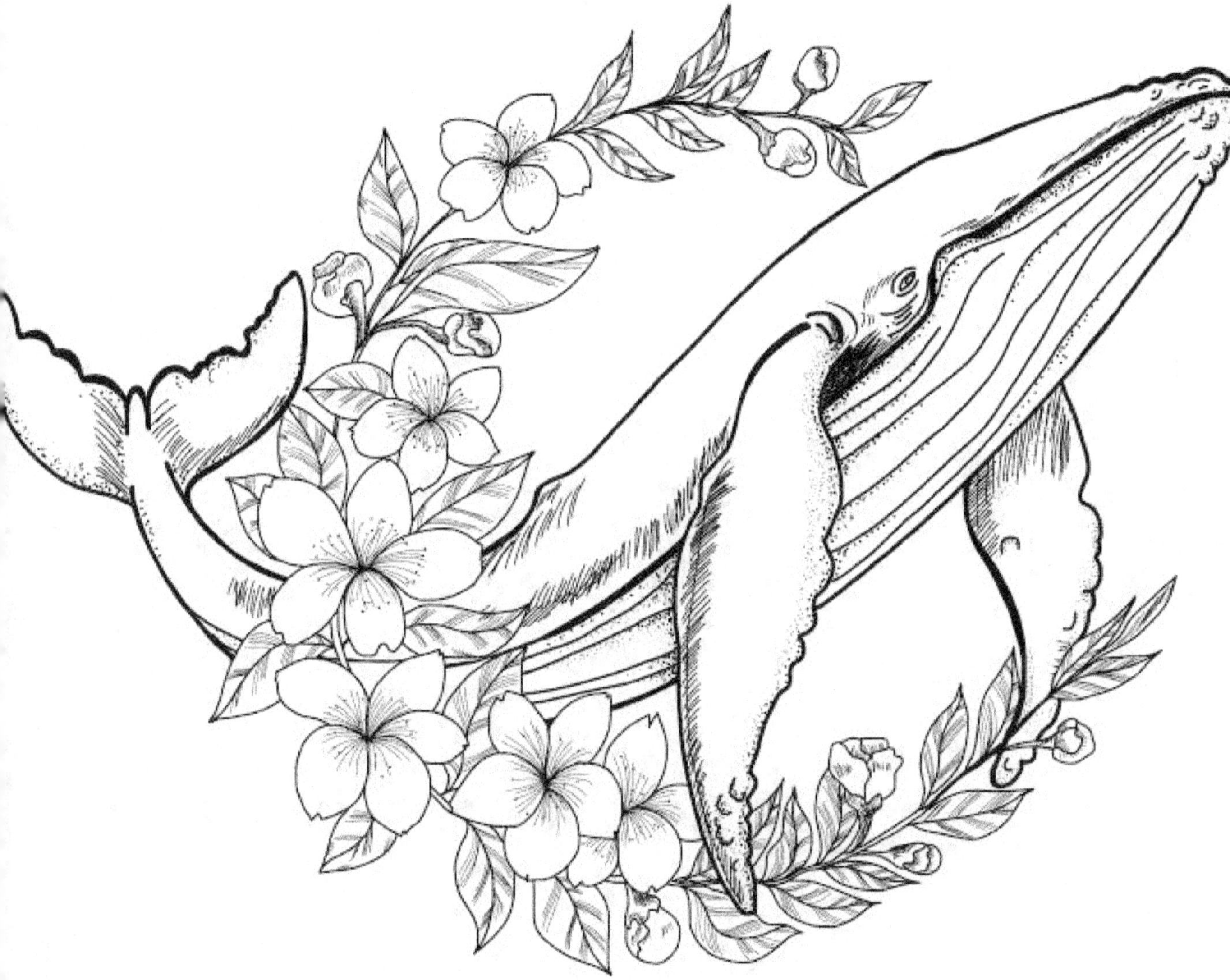

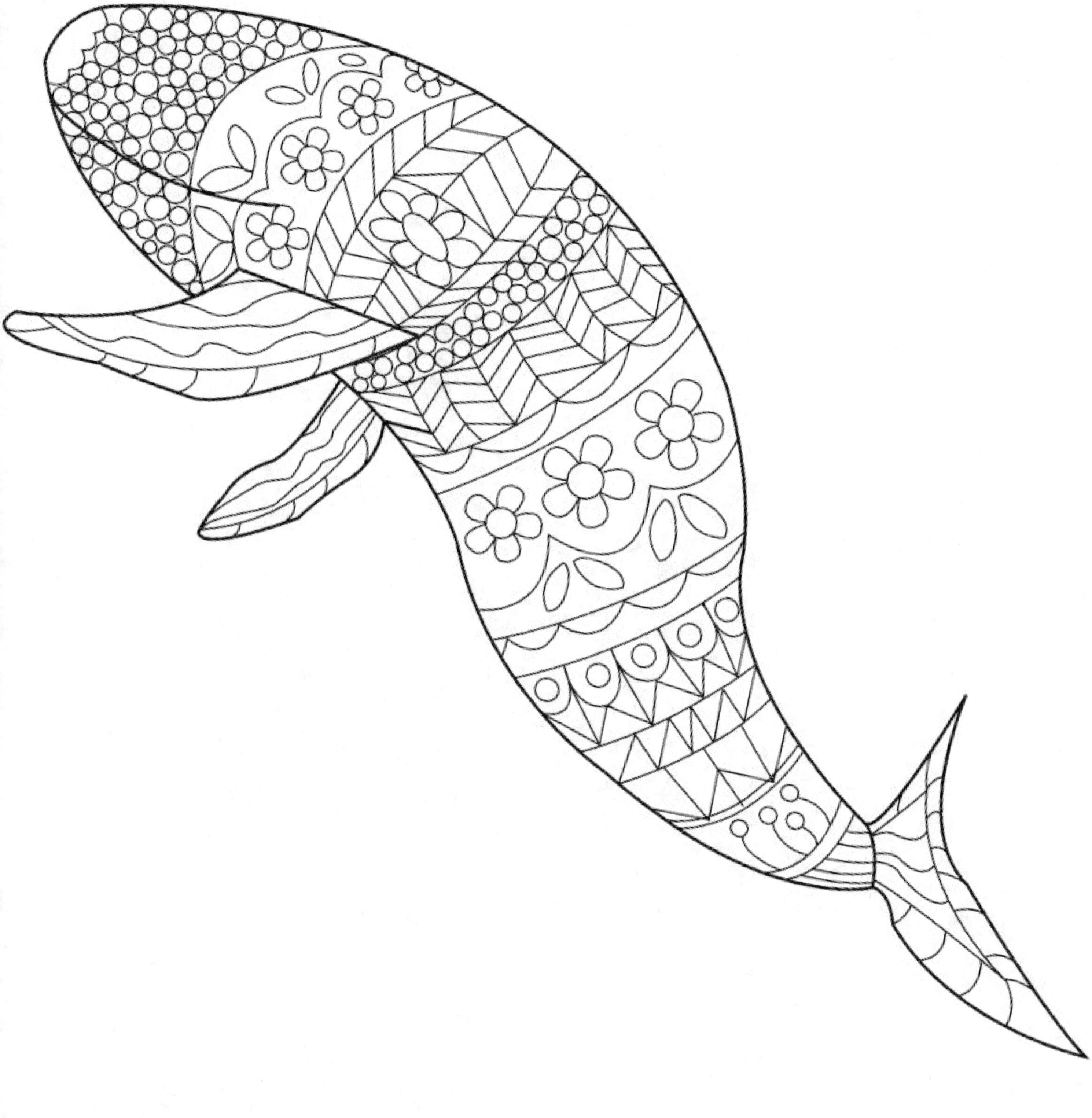

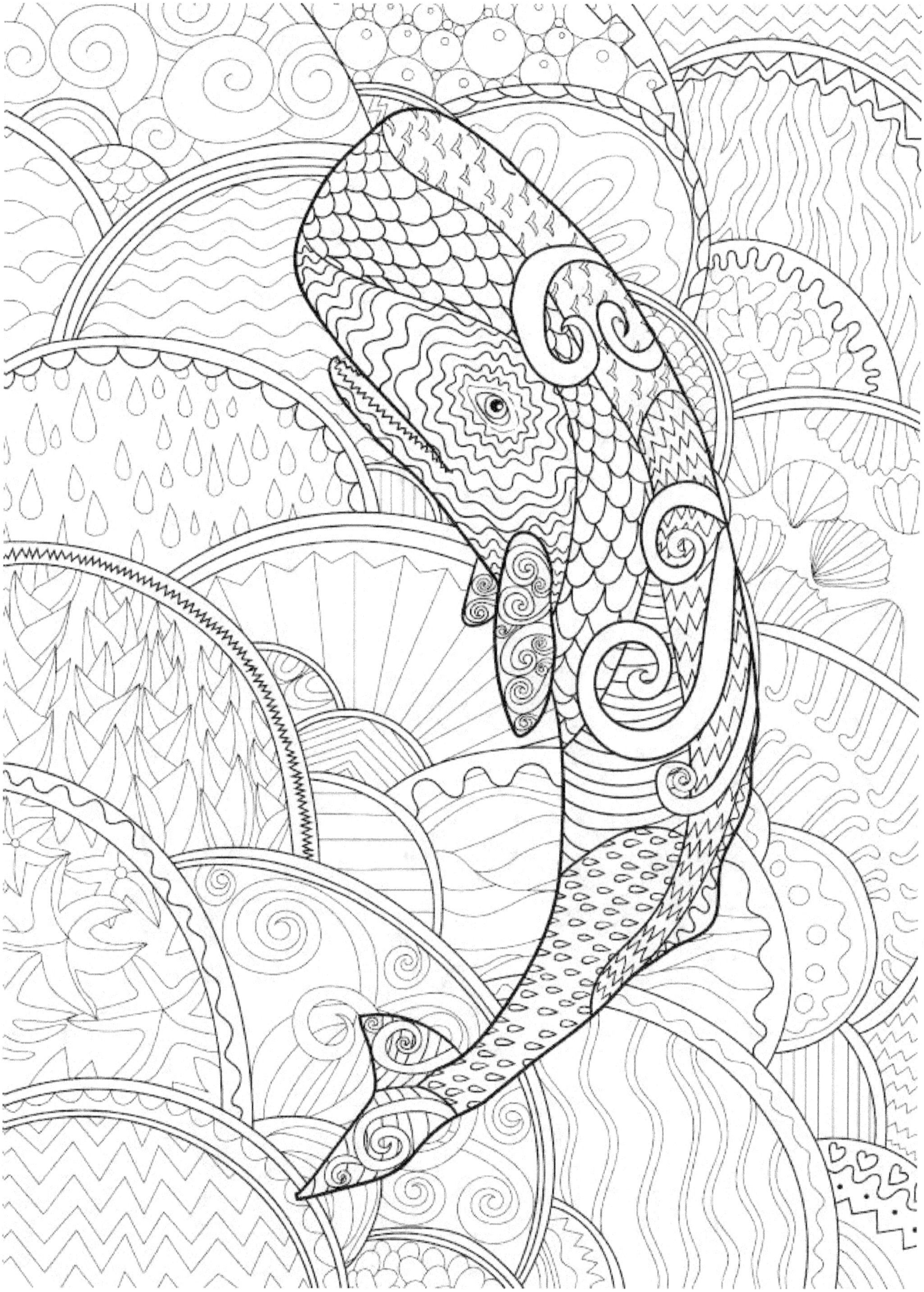

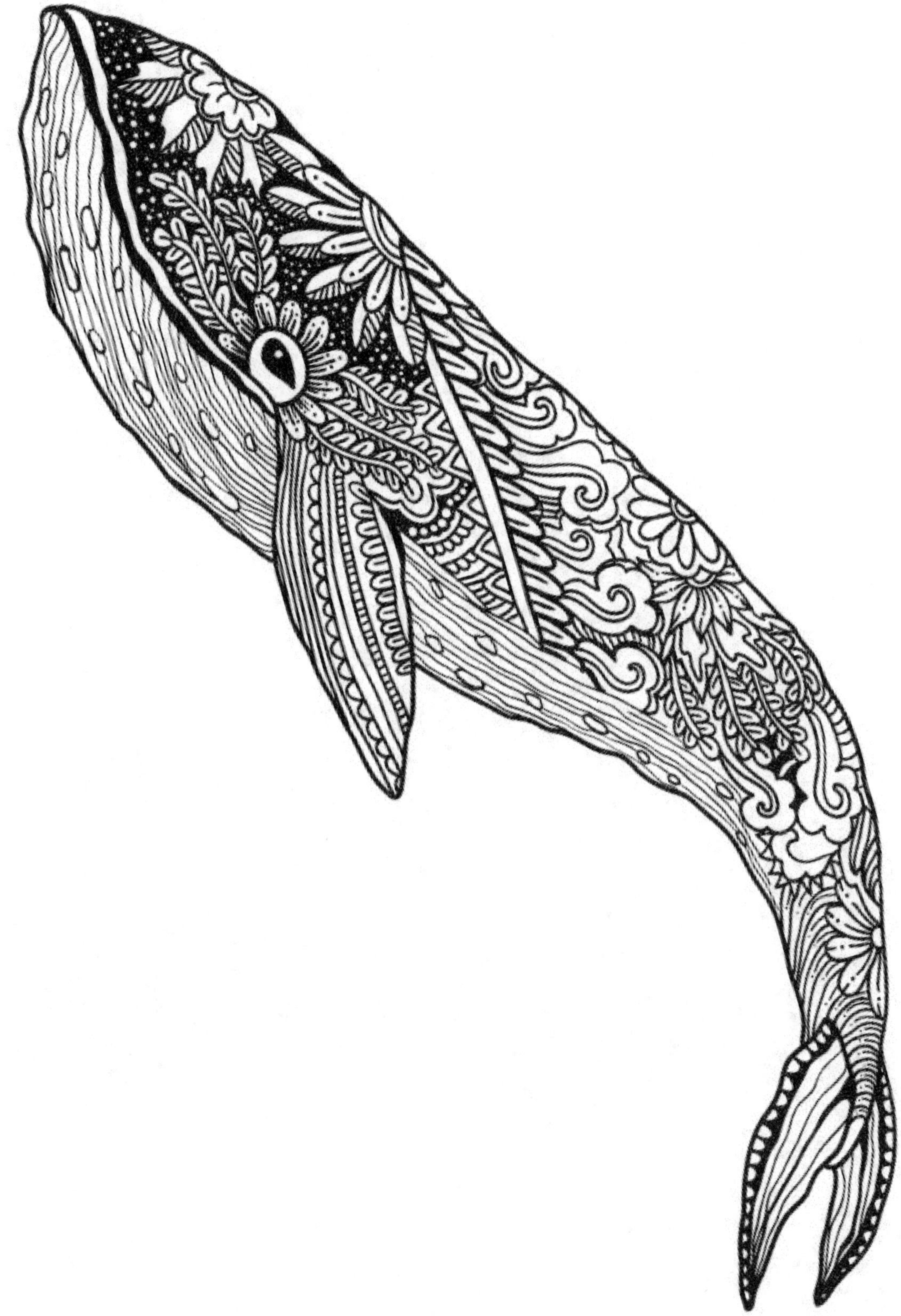

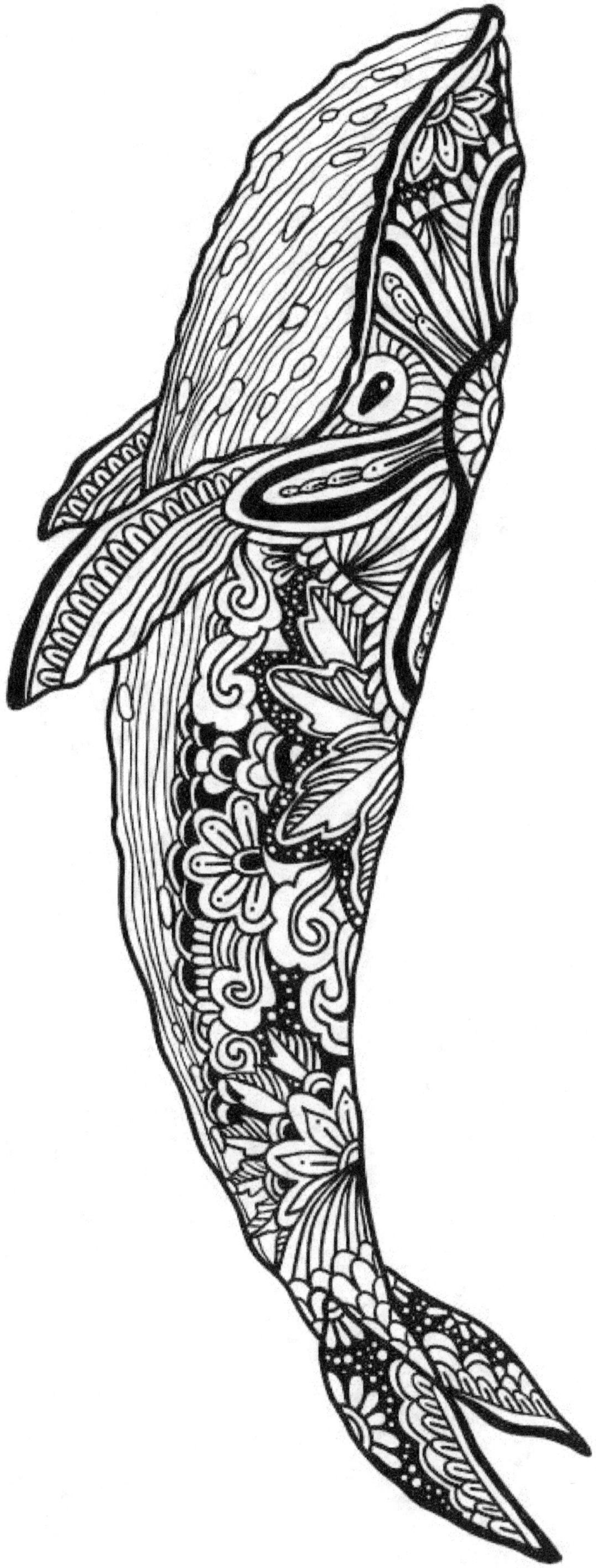

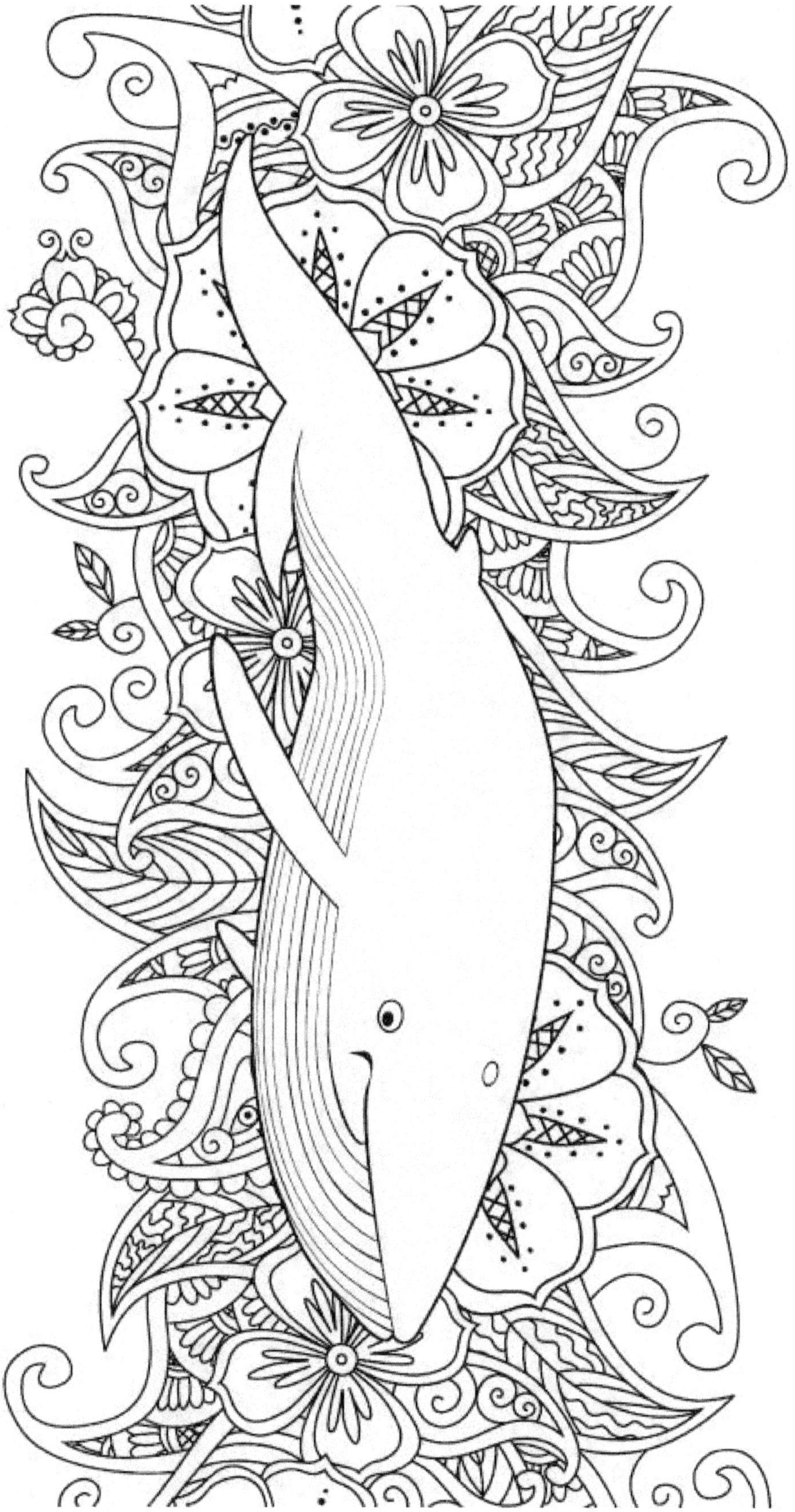

www.ingramcontent.com/pod-product-compliance
Lightning Source LLC
Chambersburg PA
CBHW081132170526
45165CB00008B/2641
* 9 7 8 1 5 4 8 1 3 4 4 1 9 *